BREAKING THE SPIRIT
OF POVERTY

All the Best "99"

Ted Montgomery

BREAKING THE SPIRIT OF POVERTY

DR. ED MONTGOMERY

BREAKING THE SPIRIT OF POVERTY by Dr. Ed Montgomery
Published by Creation House
Strang Communications Company
600 Rinehart Road
Lake Mary, FL 32746

Unless otherwise indicated, all Scripture quotations are taken from the King James Version of the Bible.

Scripture quotations marked AMP are taken from The Amplified Bible, Copyright © 1965, 1987 by The Zondervan Corporation, Grand Rapids, Michigan. Used by permission.

Scripture quotations marked NKJV are taken from The New King James Version of the Bible. Copyright © 1988 by Thomas Nelson, Inc.

Scripture quotations marked TLB are taken from The Living Bible. Copyright © 1971, 1988 by Tyndale House Publishers, Inc., Wheaton, Illinois.

Library of Congress Number: 98-73618
ISBN: 0-88419-549-X

8 9 0 1 2 3 4 5 BBG 8 7 6 5 4 3 2 1
Printed in the United States of America

DEDICATION

This book is dedicated to my grandfather, James L. Freeman, who instilled the Word of God in me from my childhood. Because of him, I never learned the meaning of the word impossible. Thank you, Daddy.

CONTENTS

Introduction . . . . *ix*

1   Magic or Management? 1

2   The Monster Must Not Reign 7

3   Prosperity:
    Good News for Poor Pews 9

4   Understanding Wealth 23

5   The Road Signs of Poverty 33

6   The Effects of Poverty
    in Black and White 51

7   God Is Not the Problem 59

8   No Curse—Just Blessing 65

9   The Unseen Force 79

10   The Power to Perform 85

11   Breaking the Spirit of Poverty 93

    Conclusion *117*

INTRODUCTION

WHY WRITE THIS BOOK?

As you know, the bookstores are loaded with books on prosperity, success, and positive thinking. I have personally read many of them and have benefited from some. Many of these financial guides are superbly written and carry a wealth of truth. Because of this, I hesitated to write this one to add it to the list. Then I noticed that very few (if any) were written from a black man's perspective. Not that a black man's view will relate any greater truth! But I do believe that the struggles of success can be seen from a different angle from my point of view. So, I wrote.

My wife and I entered the pastoral ministry in 1977. We struggled for a long time. Then we began to apply the principles written about in this book. And in 1985, with 144 members and no money in the bank, we purchased building and land worth $2.3 million. Since that time, we've opened a daycare center that teaches through the kindergarten level, a television studio, and a bookstore. We also conduct seminars that aid our people in growing spiritually, emotionally, financially, morally, and socially.

I'm not a theologian. So there will probably be some areas in this book that don't fit into certain theological frameworks. For those this may concern, I pray that you will look past my feeble attempt to accurately express my views to grasp the spirit of the message.

There is a sense of urgency within me concerning the future of the church, and her future is a glorious one indeed. She will remain strong and stable as the world systems crumble around her. This is important, because how the individual believer deals with his or her finances will determine the abundance or lack of resources within the church.

If this book inspires and gives you hope, it has accomplished its purpose.

May you prosper as you continue in His Word.

—ED MONTGOMERY

CHAPTER ONE

MAGIC OR
MANAGEMENT?

We have been awkwardly trying to raise the prosperity baby in the Christian community for some time now. This baby is still a newborn, so before I go on let me say that I strongly believe the Scriptures teach the principles of financial as well as other forms of prosperity. I believe in Psalms 1, Malachi 3:10, Luke 6:38, and 2 Corinthians 9. I believe in the law of return as well as the principle of the seed. These passages are good news to the economically oppressed.

But I also believe that many principles that have

1

been birthed under the heading of "financial prosperity" need much more developing. Whether this is the fault of the teacher or the hearer is irrelevant. A baby has been born and we must nurture that child through adolescence and into adulthood. Until then, we must continue to make the distinction between what I call "magic and management."

MAGIC OR MANAGEMENT—TRUTH OR LUCKY BREAKS?

We must never undermine the supernatural atmosphere of God's Word by implying that financial miracles don't occur. Elijah was provided for by ravens (1 Kings 17:6). Then there was the widow of Zarephath whose last bowl of meal and cruse of oil supernaturally overflowed (1 Kings 17:16). Yet another woman's vessels were supernaturally filled (2 Kings 4:3–7). Peter found his tax money in the mouth of a fish (Matt.17:24–27). Jesus multiplied the fish and the loaves (Mark 6:35–44). These were miracles, not magic. They didn't happen simply because someone spoke a few words, waved a hand, or jumped up and down.

God's supernatural, miracle-working power vs. magic is made clear in Elijah's Mount Carmel account in 1 Kings 18:20–32.

The prophets of Baal used every emotional and acrobatic stunt possible. But after all was said and done, there was still no answer from their god. Then Elijah merely called upon Jehovah, and the miraculous happened! God met Elijah's need supernaturally.

2

Christians aren't, however, commanded to walk by miracles. We are commanded to walk by faith. In between our experiences of the miraculous there must be development, cultivation, and management. That's why Paul writes:

> Now he that ministereth seed to the sower both minister bread for your food, and multiply your seed sown, and increase the fruits of your righteousness; being enriched in every thing to all bountifulness, which causeth through us thanksgiving to God.
> —2 CORINTHIANS 9:10–11

Notice Paul's phrase ". . . seed to the sower." In this passage it is assumed that the person who receives seed is able to manage the activity of sowing. To add to this, Jesus related in one of His parables:

> . . . thou hast been faithful over a few things, I will make thee ruler over many things: enter thou into the joy of thy lord.
> —MATTHEW 25:21

MANAGEMENT, NOT MAGIC

So, the Word of God strikes a strong balance between receiving from God and managing what we receive. What is received from the hand of God and how it is received depends upon relationship. We must teach the poor as well as the rich that biblical principles concerning financial prosperity aren't just magical words. Scripture isn't a list of incantations which, when spoken, will bring cars, houses, and diamonds from outer space. Fire from heaven can come, but to expect it when God expects you to strike a match can be very self-defeating.

Yes, God did speak and the earth brought forth. But there was purpose, direction, order, and management behind His spoken Word. After everything was spoken into existence, God brought forth man to manage and develop what He made. So men must understand that what God gives—must be managed and maintained.

One of the first steps out of what I have seen to be a magic-word-instant-success-mentality that many Christians have adopted, is to get people to look at what they already have. When God called Moses, one of the first questions He asked was, "What is that in thine hand?" (Exod. 4:2.) We must learn to ask ourselves, "What do I own? What has God given me? Am I using what I have to the best of my ability?" Even if people have very little to manage, asking these questions instead of looking at what they don't have—can put them in position to receive answers from God.

The 10, 10, and 80 Plan

God may suggest what I call "the 10, 10, and 80 plan," that is, give away 10 percent (tithe), save 10 percent (personal savings) and live on 80 percent. This can cause many to be more creative and inventive, find jobs, get more education, go into areas of self-employment, or merely alter their present lifestyles.

Secondly, I believe we must tell people that

not everyone is going to be a millionaire. Although I believe God doesn't want His people to live under the constant pressure of debt, I'm also aware that there are other choices people make for the kingdom's sake.

For instance, there are some people who are at their best in low-income surroundings. There are missionaries who choose to live certain lifestyles in order to reach a certain segment of society. Many of God's servants choose to live at low economic levels and are quite comfortable. They have their reasons and convictions and we can't impose upon that. Whether we agree with their theology or not, it's their choice.

My main concern is that we teach Scripture for what it is—God's Word breathed into the lives of spiritually impoverished men! It's not magic! It is the power, life, and Spirit of God. So we must teach that God's Word is not a machine that produces $20 bills.

The Word of God is alive with living principles that should motivate us to act. So we must teach that with God's Word comes the call for responsible action, and that men and women must carefully develop every thing God has given.

As God's people learn to walk in miracles—and management—they will experience a prosperity that will withstand every storm.

But if the church is ever to raise the prosperity baby we have birthed, the wisdom of God will have to be used to manage what He has given. We must stunt the growth of the "magical kingdom" concept or doom succeeding generations to ride the roller coaster of plastic prosperity.

CHAPTER TWO

THE MONSTER
MUST NOT REIGN

Greed is a monster with an insatiable appetite. Its thirst is never satisfied. After the meal it just devoured and drained, it hesitates only until another comes along. It is a monster that people can do without. So we must be taught to guard against it. In an age when greed has run rampant, believers must be in control of their potentially greedy emotions and desires. We must be reminded that prosperity is only a part of our inheritance in Christ—not an entity unto itself.

Jesus once met a young man. By today's

standards, that young man would probably be considered "upwardly mobile." He was goal-oriented, highly motivated, and approached Jesus to inquire about eternal life. So Jesus, in turn, questioned him concerning the law and the principles of God's Word. The young man had no problems with that. It was part of his upbringing. Yet, when Jesus told him to sell all his possessions and follow Him, the young man wasn't willing to exchange his life for the "Life" of God. He was rich, and wealth had become his idol in life.

We aren't told in Scripture about the plans Jesus had for this young man. We do know, however, that few were invited to follow the Lord as one of His disciples and that this is what Jesus offered. And we know that Jesus' plans were altered. Why? Because of greed. This man had another god, and his god cost him true life.

Jesus doesn't require every man to sell all his possessions. He does, however, demand total dependence upon Him as our source. This must be a clear message to all who would follow Him. We must preach it and teach it with absolute, uncompromised clarity.

The point to be made in this short yet crucial chapter is: Poverty isn't clearly seen as an off-spring of greed, but it's there, secretly lurking in the shadows. And if prosperity is to take root in God's people, greed must be reckoned with.

CHAPTER THREE

PROSPERITY: GOOD NEWS FOR POOR PEWS

Prosperity! The word sends visions of dollar signs dancing in the heads of many. Don't be alarmed at the use of the word. Jesus said that part of His mission was to "Preach the gospel to the poor." And what is the gospel? It's good news. So Jesus preached good news to the poor!

What is good news to poor people? It is the message of freedom from the pressure and oppression of poverty. Freedom from poordom! And I can tell you that this was good news to me! It was the best of reports when I learned that

God doesn't choose some people to live in the fullness of life while others remain in bondage. When I came to the realization that there were no cultural, ethnic, or racial barriers in God's economy, this good news set me free. God responds to faith, anyone's faith. Therefore, I learned that He would respond to my faith, and this liberated me!

SOME POVERTY FACTS

In 1950, one out of twelve Americans lived below the poverty line. That's twenty-two to twenty-three million Americans. In 1979, the gap widened. One out of nine Americans lived below the poverty line. That's twenty-six to twenty-seven million Americans.

You would think our many advances in technology, social reform, and higher education could bring people who live below the poverty line to a position of being able to provide for themselves. Not so!

As I update this book (1998), 15.8 percent of individual Americans, and 13.4 percent of American families still live below the poverty line. We are only aware of these people because their numbers are based on welfare, unemployment, and tax return records. If we were to add the people who don't file taxes or who have been dropped from unemployment records because their benefits have run out, the number would increase even more.

More than one fourth of all American children live in poverty. Fifty-one percent of all black children under six live in poverty. Yes! Fifty-one percent! Based on these statistics, the future looks very dim, especially for minorities.

In 1984, social welfare spending (social security, aid for families with dependent children, unemployment insurance, supplemental security income, worker's compensation and food stamps) controlled 63 percent of the federal budget. Though the numbers have been decreasing over the past four years, something is very wrong. There must be another way toward prosperity.

PROSPERITY—WHAT IS IT?

To many Americans, prosperity is owning a house and two cars with a comfortable income, and a good retirement plan for future leisure. I call this the "Leave it to Beaver" image. (*Leave it to Beaver* was a TV sitcom that portrayed a typical upper-middle-income family in the '50s that never had any serious problems.)

But there is another image of prosperity: God's image.

The Word of God says:

> I have been young, and now am old; yet have I not seen the righteous forsaken, nor his seed begging bread.
> —PSALMS 37:25

There is a relationship of prosperity for every family member in the house of God. When the Word of God is studied from a view of providence, Christians will begin to understand that

11

God takes care of His own. God's relationship of prosperity extends even to the children and grandchildren of those who trust Him. But if we are to ever receive these blessings, God's people must understand God's image of prosperity.

According to the Word of God, prosperity is the state in which one is having all of his needs met by Jehovah (God).

One of the redemptive names of God revealed to Abraham was El Shaddai. This name, according to one translation, means "The Breast." God likened Himself to a woman's breast after she gives birth to a child. As a child draws its nourishment from the mother, so we as believers must draw our nourishment from the Person of God— all our nourishment.

Human beings have a variety of needs. These needs are mental, emotional, moral, social, physical, and financial. Why didn't I include spiritual? Because all of the needs I mentioned emanate from the spiritual. So, a biblical view of prosperity ensures that all of your needs are supplied in every area.

For years we have dwelt on God meeting the emotional, mental, and social needs. But what about the financial? Is God willing to get involved? He most certainly is! I believe God's Word reveals some explicit instructions concerning economics. It was this belief that opened my eyes to some interesting principles.

THE BEGINNING

In 1976, my wife, Sandra, and I left Cleveland,

Ohio, with our daughter Angela and moved to Dallas, Texas. The move alone cost us every penny we had. But we were determined to make it work. I was a young preacher who believed that God would take care of us, though I had never really tested that belief in any specific area.

In Dallas I found a job which barely paid the rent. So it wasn't long before our expenses caught up with and passed our weekly income. I'll never forget the day my wife told me that we had eaten our last meal. Dinner time was approaching, but we had no money and no relative to run to for help.

That day I really began to pray. Of course, I always prayed. Prayer wasn't unusual for me. After all, I was a preacher! But this time was different. Instead of complaining to God about our situation, I began by rehearsing all the Scripture I knew about God's provision. Then I reminded God that according to His Word, He was obligated to care of His own. Little did I know at the time that this was called "praying in faith."

I got up from my knees, called my wife, and told her to get ready for dinner. Then I explained that I was going out and would be back with something for dinner. I went to visit my pastor's house. I really don't remember why, but I do know that I didn't plan to tell him my financial situation. I was trusting God completely.

As I walked through the door of my pastor's house I was told he wasn't home, and his wife invited me in. The next few moments were unforgettable. She explained to me that she had a problem. It seemed that everyone had other plans and that no one in the family would be home for dinner that night. She had thawed out a chicken and no one would be there to eat it. Then she said if my wife hadn't cooked yet, would I please take the chicken off her hands.

She also threw in a few canned goods to make a complete dinner! I composed myself outwardly, but there were about a thousand "Thank you, Jesus" praises bubbling up in my spirit!

Now tell me, was this an accident, a coincidence, or was it God? I know it to be the latter! That chicken was the tastiest chicken I've ever eaten. It came straight from the hand of God. I learned that my faith did work! God did provide!

On another occasion, I had just been called to pastor a church in a small town. The town was sixty miles away. At the time I owned a 1969 Oldsmobile. And wouldn't you know that the car decided to stop functioning just when I needed it most?

What was I going to do? Well, you guessed it— I figured if God could provide a chicken, He could also provide a car!

I remembered how I prayed for food and tried the same type of prayer again. Only this time I got up and went to look for a car instead of food. I walked to the nearest dealership and into the head man's office, told him my situation, and guess what? He turned me down! I was young with no job and had no credit history. This little setback tried to destroy my faith, but I wouldn't let it.

The next morning when I got up, I sensed a small voice inside telling me to try starting my old junk-heap. So I went downstairs, opened the hood of the car, twisted a few wires, and lo and behold—it started up! As I closed the door, I noticed that there were three red lights flashing on the dash board. They were telling me that something was wrong with the engine (as if I didn't know). I knew if I turned the car off it wouldn't start again. So I hurriedly put it in gear and drove off. To this day I'm not sure where I had decided to go, I just drove.

After driving about twenty minutes and exhausting most of my fuel, I spotted a tan 1974 Buick sitting in a gas station with a "for sale" sign in the window. As I drove into the station, I left the motor running for fear of not being able to start the car again.

I asked about that Buick I had seen. The man I was talking to was the car owner, and he was staring at me strangely. He eventually asked if I had ever preached at a certain church. I told him I had. He asked me what church I was going to start pastoring. I told him the name of it and that I needed a car to get there. Then I learned (as it just so happened) that his brother-in-law was one of the deacons there.

He had me pull my old junk-heap to the back, shut it off, and come to the office. When I came in, he told me to get in the '74 Buick and go for a ride with him. I felt like a king with a new kingdom!

After about ten minutes, he told me to turn into a driveway. It was a bank. Then he told me to get out and go in with him. Thirty minutes later, we walked out of that bank—and I owned that car!

That man, who had never met me in his life, co-signed for me at the bank. Was this an accident, a coincidence, or was it God? It was God! God had once again financially provided.

In the years that followed I pondered these events and eventually learned the scriptural principle behind the prayer I prayed:

> . . . What things soever ye desire, when ye pray, believe that ye receive them, and ye shall have them.
>
> —MARK 11:24

I also learned that even though prosperity is available to every believer, not every believer acts upon this principle of praying according to Scripture and acting in faith. These events were to serve as a reminder concerning God's faithfulness to His Word for the rest of my life.

God is El Shaddai. He does meet every need—even financial ones!

THE MOVE

After I pastored that country church for three-and-one-half years, I sensed God telling me it was time to move on. So with our belongings, $500, and a lot of faith, we moved to Houston, Texas. We had never been to Houston, and we knew no one there. But we acted upon what we believed to be a word from God revealed in our spirit.

This was an exciting step of faith. Within two weeks we had exhausted all of our resources. We were trusting God to provide again, and, praise

God, He did. My wife found a job at a day care center, and I started working as an office supply salesman. I don't have to tell you it was tough, but I think I will anyway. Hey! It was tough! Just like many people, we had to trust God for car payments, light, telephone, and grocery bills! Every week we felt pressure. The money was going out as fast as it came in, but God saw us through.

Now let me interject something at this point. Although we felt led to Houston, to build a church, Sandra and I never sat back unemployed (by choice) waiting on God to supply. The apostle Paul said:

> For even when we were with you, this we commanded you, that if any would not work, neither should he eat.
> —2 Thessalonians 3:10

I had to put my hand to something for God to prosper it, because being called of God doesn't exempt us from work. I'll deal with that more fully in a later chapter.

We had been in Houston for several months before the Lord finally released us to start the church. It was in the building of the ministry that we saw many financial miracles, one right after another. (And many testings of our faith, I might add!)

For instance, we started our church in August of 1981 with zero members. We leased eighteen hundred square feet of space in a one-story office strip center. We signed a two-year lease of $1000 a month. At this point you probably think I was crazy! Looking back, I'm inclined to agree! But you have to remember, we had never started a church before. (I didn't find out until later that we had leased space in one of the most expensive areas of Houston and that we could have started in another section of town at a much lower cost.)

But we were the only predominately black church (and I use the term "black church" for identification purposes only) within a radius of six miles. We were on the edge of Houston's proposed expansion. So God knew what He was doing.

Remember, our rent was $1000 a month. We had no members, we were out of money, and the rent was due again in thirty days. But praise God! Within thirty days we had fifteen members and God provided the $1000—just in the nick of time, I might add! I was to learn over the next few years that faith made nothing easy. It only made things possible.

For two years our congregational numbers resembled a roller coaster. They went up and down, up and down! Overall we grew to about eighty— or so I thought!

IDEAS + ABILITY + WORK = MONEY

Then in July of 1983, we were given the opportunity to move into larger facilities in another office building, this time on the second floor. This move gave us 9,600 square feet and a monthly lease of $4300! We started with eighty, but moved in with only fifty people. (I later learned that with every move of a congregation you have a tendency to lose some. I don't know why, it just happens.) Again, God provided the finances each month, but this time it took almost a year-and-one-half before we started seeing money over and above the rent. We grew tremendously during that period. The growth wasn't numerical, but our faith in the ability of God to provide exploded tremendously! Deuteronomy 8:18 became alive to us:

> But thou shalt remember the Lord thy God: for it is he that giveth thee power to get wealth, that he may establish his covenant which he sware unto thy fathers, as it is this day.

From this passage God gave us a unique spiritual principle: Ideas + Ability + Work = Money. (I'll expand on this later.)

We worked that principle individually and as a corporate body. Many times it looked as if we weren't going to make it. At some of the most crucial financial times, members would leave. To this day it isn't very clear why they left. We just dug a little deeper into our faith in God, and God saw us through.

After about a year-and-one-half we were easily able to pay our rent, and we were planning some other things. In January of 1985, we were about to undertake one of the greatest moves of faith in our history. God had opened the door for us to purchase $2.5 million worth of buildings and property.

In the natural, we only had 144 members; we

had no money in the bank; and we had no down payment to offer. But somehow we knew it was God's leading! We had learned over the years that every time we became financially comfortable, God called us to a greater step of faith.

I believe there is a principle to grasp here. I've learned that we can't rest on past financial victories. We can't come to a point (that Jesus described in a parable) where we can say, "Soul take thy rest, eat, drink, and be merry." Poverty will come if we ever allow ourselves to slip into this kind of thinking that says, "I have gotten myself this wealth." So we must always remember that God is the Giver and Source of life. And His life produces, daily, whatever is necessary to meet our needs.

In July of 1985, we moved into that $2.5 million property. With 144 members we possessed our land and began to maintain it. To this day we haven't stopped using our faith. We still trust God to provide our financial needs. And He does! We keep our eyes and ears open because He provides in so many various ways! God is truly unique!

Since those early days our congregation has grown tremendously. We have moved into publishing, we have a day care center and an early learning center for children, we're on television, and much more. I must add that God didn't provide the money up front. Nor did we jump off into a lot of debt and beg God to help us catch up. God provided for us as we took each step of faith, working daily with us!

In the coming chapters I am going to share some biblical principles involving poverty and prosperity with you. Please don't see these things as some "abra kadabra" magical formula. See them for what they are—principles from God's Word. And don't put great stock in my application of the principles. Set your faith like concrete in the Word of God, because it is your faith and trust that will cause you to prosper.

But before we move on, let me say that all of the accomplishments I've shared with you are only the highlights of certain time periods. It is not my intention to give the impression that every moment was smooth sailing. Nor do I mean to imply that buildings and land are the primary signs of prosperity. On the contrary, these things I've relayed to you show my own overcoming of many struggles, fears, doubts, tense moments, and near failures.

Prosperity must be seen in the determination of a people to succeed despite obstacles. So, to remain as close to my subject as possible, I haven't provided an exhaustive version of how we moved from point "A" to point "Z."

At some point in the future God will release me to tell the "complete" story, maybe an autobiography. But my main goal in this book is to assure you that financial prosperity is possible and available, and that God is no respecter of persons. It can happen for anyone who trusts Him. I know this to be true, because it happened for me.

CHAPTER FOUR

UNDERSTANDING WEALTH

> But thou shalt remember the Lord thy God: for it is he that giveth thee power to get wealth, that he may establish his covenant which he sware unto thy fathers, as it is this day.
>
> —DEUTERONOMY 8:18

The most common definition of wealth has catapulted many into an unending quest for security. This is unfortunate because those who do this view wealth in terms of money only. This is a great deception. Although money is certainly a part of wealth, money is not wealth in itself.

I see the biblical view of wealth as: Being provided for through an unlimited supply. So wealth should be viewed in light of a present need, and money may not be that need. A need may consist of physical healing, peace of mind, direction, or purpose. This means a person can be physically, mentally, or motivationally poverty stricken.

Many times we forget that God's ultimate will for us is complete wholeness; spirit, soul, and body. So financial wealth is not an end in itself. God dealt with man in the Old Testament to develop both physical and spiritual wholeness. Physical health, disciplined children, financial resources, and a good name were all considered as signs that Jehovah had His hand on an individual. But again, financial wealth was only one of these areas.

I believe this is where the teaching of prosperity has caused some ripples throughout the body of Christ. Many well-meaning people have taught and heard the "prosperity message" as representing an ultimate end. The same is true of salvation in some circles. Many get caught up in only bringing people to the place of being born again. This, of course, is primary and wonderful. But salvation is more than the new birth alone. It is also discipleship. To teach new birth alone and make it an end of itself robs the believer of maturity, and we are expected to grow up.

The same is true of prosperity. If we are only teaching financial well-being, believers will never grow up. So prosperity can't begin, nor should it end, with money. Money is just a fraction of the biblical teaching on prosperity.

As a matter of fact, some areas of financial poverty can be erased by a simple attitude adjustment. With the right attitude, God can prosper men in many areas. They may see immediate results through new job interviews, increased sales, and the increased energy level it takes to go into business. When Jesus healed He said, "Be made whole (complete)."

Wealth is a whole-man principle because God's unlimited supply flows into every area of life. But since we're primarily dealing with money in this book, we will also apply prosperity's concept of "unlimited supply."

When we exhaust our search for an unlimited supply (wealth), we will ultimately come face to face with God. Isaiah 45:3 says:

> And I will give thee the treasures of darkness, and hidden riches of secret places, that thou mayest know that I, the Lord, which call thee by thy name, am the God of Israel.

Several years ago, I watched a movie about the great Gold Rush of the nineteenth century. It told the story of men who packed up their families and headed for the hills of California to strike it rich. The majority of the people found little more than dreams, and since dreams didn't keep food on the table, they gave up and went back home. Some stayed, and every now and then would find a seemingly unlimited vein of gold. They called these veins "glory holes." I believe this is what God calls the "riches of secret places." God knows where the "glory holes" are!

I'm not advocating that you begin to dig around in your backyard! You may hit a water pipe, and that will cost you! What I am saying is there are vehicles of wealth that God will show you if you will learn how to plug into Him!

The Word says:

> The secret things belong unto the Lord our
> God: but those things which are revealed
> belong unto us and to our children for ever,
> that we may do all the words of this law.
> —DEUTERONOMY 29:29

The things God reveals belong to us! So if God reveals a hidden source of wealth, it belongs to His people!

Now notice the other part of this verse ". . . that we may do all the words of this law [spiritual laws]."

COVENANT

Many times we only view the Scriptures as God talking to us individually. And of course, we must receive the Bible as personal. But we must also look at God's dealing with Israel from a historic point of view. As you study the historic accounts you will see that God was building a nation, and that through that nation God planned to manifest Himself. Therefore, God's people had great responsibilities. And one of those responsibilities involved providing for the continuance of the nation. To achieve this, finances were needed. God dealt with them through law, including the issue of money. But the end of the Law was always intended to instill a relationship through love. And love relationship is based on covenant.

Jehovah deals with His people based on covenant, which though unconditional in receiving forgiveness, was based on provisions of faithful obedience. God promised to provide for His people. In return, His people were commanded to use their resources to support the extension of God's kingdom in the earth.

Paul writes of our New Testament covenant in Ephesians 4:28–29:

> Let him that stole steal no more: but rather let him labour, working with his hands the thing which is good, that he may have to give to him that needeth. Let no corrupt communication proceed out of your mouth, but that which is good to the use of edifying, that it may minister grace unto the hearers.

So, God provides for those who are in covenant with Him, knowing that they will continue to further His will toward other men on the earth. We receive from God so we may have our own needs met, move the gospel, relieve the poor, and establish godly principles on the earth. This is the reason and purpose connected with biblical wealth.

MONEY

Although I have already given a covenant definition of wealth, the image of money probably still pops up. So let's not suppress it—let's deal with it.

Have you ever heard someone say, "I don't know what happens to my money; it just keeps getting away from me"? Well, contrary to what people think, money doesn't have legs. Money is an inanimate object that has no force of its own. It is amoral, neither good nor bad. Still, it does move.

I see money flowing into pornography, X-rated movies, abortion, drug trafficking, away from the poor and into the hands of the rich. This tells me that there is some force involved. But if money can flow into the cancers of our society, why can't it be moved into the healthy areas of life?

First we must ask: "What is the force that causes money to flow?" The answer is: "People!" That's right—people! Whatever motivates people also motivates the direction in which money flows. If evil is the motivating force, then money will flow into the vehicles of evil. But if good is the motivating force, money can flow into the machinery that generates cures for sickness and comfort for the destitute.

So, I think I've made my point. Money has no ears, legs, or arms. It doesn't hear us, it can't run or "get away" from us, and it certainly can't see us. Money doesn't see race, culture, or the color of one's skin. Racism and prejudice exist in our society, but there are those of every race who experience financial freedom—and financial bondage.

Education has some value, but we know there are rich people who have never finished high school or college.

Hard work is commendable, but many people work hard all of their lives and stay continually poor.

Going to church is good but is no guarantee that you will prosper. If you violate certain principles, money won't flow in your direction.

So, regardless of race, religion, or educational status, money will or won't flow, based on an individual's situation.

When I speak of "money" I'm talking in terms of what other people will accept in exchange for something else. Things of value can't be viewed in terms of paper money only. The value of paper money goes up and down. Why? Those who move it make it so. This fluctuation is caused by human beings. So never place complete trust in the value of paper money. Money is backed by a monetary standard that its movers adjust on any given day.

IN THE BEGINNING . . . GOLD AND PRECIOUS STONES

Speaking of Adam and Eve's original environment, the Bible says:

> The name of the first is Pison: That is it which compasseth the whole land of Havilah, where there is gold; And the gold of that land is good: there is bdellium and the onyx stone.
>
> —GENESIS 2:11–12

Gold and precious stones are mentioned quickly in the Bible. The minerals listed in the beginning were called "good" because they were pure. There were no alloys or mixtures. It was God who first placed value upon these minerals, and their original value was purely aesthetic. These stones were valued for their beauty. They reflected the beauty and glory of God.

Today, gold and precious stones are valued for what they can buy. Precious stones and minerals don't have intrinsic value, because anything that has intrinsic value can't be affected by external circumstances such as fire, flood, tricks, or schemes. Therefore, gold is valuable because man puts value on it. God is the only one who has intrinsic value, and He isn't moved by the whims and changes of society.

Job 27:16–17 says:

> Though he heap up silver as the dust, and prepare raiment as the clay; he may prepare it, but the just shall put it on, and the innocent shall divide the silver.

When our motivation is plugged into God—who has intrinsic value—He is able to do great things with money through us. With the proper motivation paper money in the hands of God's people can be turned back into that which reflects the beauty and glory of God.

And what gives God glory? Good works that have the life force of God as their motivation. Jesus said, "Let your light so shine before men, that they may see your good works, and glorify your Father which is in heaven" (Matthew 5:16).

When we take care of the poor and elderly, heal the sick, liberate the drug addict, educate our children mentally and spiritually, provide opportunities for work, and give purpose, meaning and direction to life, we make visible the glory of God!

So remember, wealth is for wholeness, it is

based on covenant, and can flow through trusting hands to do good works upon the earth. This is what Jesus meant when He preached:

> The Spirit of the Lord [is] upon Me, because He has anointed Me [the Anointed One, the Messiah] to preach the good news (the gospel) to the poor; He has sent Me to announce release to the captives and recovery of sight to the blind, to send forth as delivered those who are oppressed [who are downtrodden, bruised, crushed and broken down by calamity].
>
> —LUKE 4:18, AMP

CHAPTER FIVE

THE ROAD SIGNS
OF POVERTY

P overty is not living in a ghetto or growing up in the most run-down part of town. Being poor doesn't come as a result of high unemployment or the lack of qualifying skills. These things are merely the fruit of poverty, not its root.

So what is poverty? Poverty is a destructive spirit, an intangible force, an alien entity that robs human beings of their dreams, goals, motivations, and desires. Poverty comes right from the pit of hell! Remember, "being broke" is only a temporary condition, but poverty is a spirit.

POVERTY IS A SPIRIT

Have you ever heard the term "poverty-stricken"? Of course! This alludes to the concept that poverty is something that comes upon a person, a group of people, a community, or a nation. The devastation caused by poverty affects more than the pockets; it affects the whole man.

Poverty is nearly always connected with unrighteousness. It was the unrighteousness of an individual or the unrighteousness of the entire nation that brought oppression upon the people of Israel.

In the case of the widow at Zarephath (1 Kings 17:8–16), her poverty was the result of God's judgment upon the rule of Ahab. Ahab had allowed the entrance of idol worship into the land, and this spiritual problem brought physical destitution.

For years, America's political leaders have advocated social programs: welfare, aid, work programs, and job training programs. But tell me, why haven't these programs eradicated poverty in a nation as affluent as ours? Why is it that some remain in poverty while others rise above it? I submit that the problem goes beyond environment. There is a spirit involved. It sweeps through cultures and communities. I also submit that if we can expose poverty as a spirit, then we can introduce the liberating power of the gospel as the answer to its destructive power.

The word *poverty* or *poor* as it is recorded in the Greek text means "to be a beggar." In the day of the apostle Paul, the streets of Greece would be lined with people whose sole occupation was to beg from others. Nowhere does the Bible tell us that it is God's will for a man to be in poverty. There is nothing "holy" about being poor.

The signs of poverty can be easily recognized when you know what to look for. Some say, "The fact that I don't have enough money is sign enough!" But remember that I said being poor is a spirit and not just a lack of money.

Let me explain. Since poverty is intertwined with the attitude of an individual, you can easily understand what I mean when I say that a person can earn $100 million and still be in poverty because he spends $99 million. So poverty possesses more characteristics than just a "lack" of money. There are seven of these characteristics, or signs, that I know of. Let's look at them in order.

POVERTY SIGN # 1: REFUSING INSTRUCTION

Poverty and shame come to him who refuses instruction and correction, but he who heeds reproof is honored.
—PROVERBS 13:18, AMP

If you want to be free from a poverty spirit, you have to be teachable. God has given certain instructions to get people out of poverty, but they do absolutely no good if they aren't listened to, learned, and acted upon.

One Christmas I had the pleasure of putting my daughter's bicycle together. Did I say pleasure? It could have been anyway, that is if I followed the directions. Now I really believed that I had the ingenuity to put that contraption together without the instructions! But after I was done, there were several parts left with no place to put them. Needless to say that by then, I knew I wasn't the engineering genius I had thought myself to be! I tried to fit this and that wherever it would, because I thought I knew bikes! When I was halfway finished I knew . . . I should have followed the instructions! But I plodded along anyway.

Just as I had trouble putting that bicycle together, people will experience trouble putting their lives together unless they read God's instruction manual—the Bible.

> All these curses shall come upon you and shall pursue you and overtake you till you are destroyed, because you do not obey the voice of the Lord your God, to keep His commandments and His statutes which He commanded you. They shall be upon you for a sign [of warning to other nations] and for a wonder, and upon your descendants forever. Because you did not serve the Lord your God with joyfulness of [mind and] heart [in gratitude] for the abundance of all [with which He had blessed you], Therefore you shall serve your enemies whom the Lord shall send against you, in hunger and thirst, in nakedness and in want of all things; and He will put a yoke of iron upon your neck until he has destroyed you.
>
> —DEUTERONOMY 28:45–48, AMP

Unless the believer acts in faith on the Word of God, God cannot justly hold back (rebuke) the thieves of abundance. The curses spoken of in the Deuteronomy passage don't come upon you to teach you a lesson. They come because people refuse to hearken or listen to the Word (instructions) of the Lord. Think about it!

The law of traffic control says we can experience safe driving if we stop at red lights and proceed at green ones. So it isn't the fault of the city if a person proceeds on a red light and has an accident. The will of the city that puts up the lights is that its citizens experience safe and trouble-free driving.

So it is with God. His will for all people is stated in the following passage:

> And it shall come to pass, if thou shalt hearken [listen] diligently unto the voice [instructions] of the Lord thy God, to observe and to do all his commandments which I command thee this day, that the Lord thy God will set thee on high above all nations of the earth. And all these blessings shall come on thee, and overtake thee, if thou shalt hearken unto the voice of the Lord thy God.
>
> —DEUTERONOMY 28:1–2

Poverty-stricken communities are in bondage because they place their faith in the system of the world and doubt God's system for living. To some this may sound spiritually lofty. But remember, God's Word is also practical. His Word gives instructions in areas of savings, management, precautions, co-signing, debt, and many other practical financial dealings.

God has set different types of ministries in the body of Christ. He has given pastors and teachers the desire to see their people prosper. The Word says, "My people are destroyed for lack of knowledge . . ." (Hosea 4:6). So a lack of knowledge or lack of instruction causes failure. We must teach people not to close their minds and to allow God to renew their minds. A renewed mind will bring about change. It will transform individuals! (See Romans 12:1–3.)

The mind must be renewed concerning what God says about financial matters. These instructions can't be rejected. Again, Proverbs 13:18 says, "Poverty and shame shall be to him who refuses instruction." In other words, poverty will come to those who don't listen to good instructions. But the believer who listens shall be honored and promoted in life! That's a promise!

POVERTY SIGN #2: FOLLOWING VAIN PERSONS

He that tilleth his land shall have plenty of bread: but he that followeth after vain persons shall have poverty enough.
—PROVERBS 28:19

"Vain persons" in this verse refers to "empty people with empty goals." Too often believers attach themselves to people who are going no where! Matthew says:

> If two of you shall agree on earth as touching
> any thing that they shall ask, it shall be done
> for them of my Father which is in heaven.
>   —MATTHEW 18:19

Notice the phrase ". . . as touching any thing"
Anything! Now, listen, you can agree to having
doubt as well as having faith. The emphasis is on
agreement.

We often hear a lot about people who have a
desire to succeed—but are their plans and pur-
suits really concrete? I remember during my
college days hearing someone say, "If you're
going to carry someone's briefcase, make sure it's
someone who is going somewhere."

I've learned that being around people who talk
words of faith will encourage you to develop
your faith. But surrounding yourself with people
who talk doubt and unbelief will only help you
develop your doubts and unbelief. You can easily
spot people who are talking themselves right into
poverty. Usually these people:

1. Are very critical of prosperous people.

2. Are constantly looking for flaws in the
    lives of people who are achieving some-
    thing.

3. Are always complaining about how
    others always get the good breaks in
    life.

4. Believe that the world system owes them something.

God's people can't afford to attach themselves and their thinking to such empty people. God has called us to greater things.

POVERTY SIGN #3: WITHHOLDING MORE THAN YOU NEED

> . . . There is that withholdeth more than is meet, but it tendeth to poverty.
> —PROVERBS 11:24

Any person who has made a great deal of money will tell you it is necessary to invest. Investing money requires that you give up a sum of money in order to make a greater sum. So, God's people must also learn to invest, to give!

Remember, poverty isn't a condition of finances; it's a condition of the spirit. When the spirit man learns that the character of his God is good and that He wants His children to have a life of quality, faith arises in the promise that God takes care of His own.

When there is that assurance by faith, believers are able to have faith in the system God has provided to prosper His own. And giving is a part of that system. Just as turning a key is a part of the ignition system of an automobile—giving is a part of the system that leads a person out of poverty.

Giving frees the individual to receive. A person who is under the oppression of poverty is usually looking for an excuse to hold on to (grip) the little he possesses. These excuses are born out of the fear of never having enough. One common statement I've heard is, "When I get some extra money, then I'll give." This is admirable, but a very big mistake. This isn't faith in the system of God. It's a "see and then believe" type of system. And God doesn't reward doubt, He rewards faith!

Faith believes; then because of the power of that faith, it inevitably sees the results. Remember, Proverbs 11:24 says "withholding . . . tendeth [or leans] to poverty." But faith breaks that cycle of fear, and the broken cycle eliminates the excuses for withholding. From the moment giving takes place, the cycle of poverty is broken! Once the excuses are dismissed, that individual is free to give. They are then released to begin operating in another cycle—prosperity! But for the fear cycle to change, it must first be slowed down to a complete stop; then it can be turned in the opposite direction.

If a car is going forward and needs to go in reverse, then it must first come to a stop before it can change gears. The same principle operates in breaking the poverty cycle. A person may not see his ultimate financial goals realized in twenty-four hours—but things will have begun to change once he starts giving. His faith is working! God promises to respond!

> And I will rebuke the devourer [insects and plagues] for your sakes and he shall not destroy the fruits of your ground, neither shall your vine drop its fruit before the time in the field, says the Lord of hosts.
> —MALACHI 3:11, AMP

POVERTY SIGN #4: GET-RICH-QUICK MOTIVATION

Now I don't think I need to say this again, but God isn't opposed to your being rich. As a matter of fact, the Word of God is full of examples of those who became rich just because they sought after God. Follow God and: "Surely goodness and mercy shall follow you" (Psalms 23:6). When you follow the Word of God, "all these things" are added to you. What things? "Goodness and mercy shall follow you." This has always been God's message to us and this leads to prosperity.

But the Word also tells us that a get-rich-quick motivation will lead to poverty. This type of motivation is hard to detect in the beginning, but it will ultimately show up. People who have this attitude usually don't maintain their wealth very long.

You might ask, "What about the teaching of planting seeds with the motivation of giving in order to receive? Is this motive wrong?" Well, let's look at it.

There is nothing wrong with giving in order to receive. I repeat: There is nothing wrong with giving in order to receive! After all, this is God's system of supplying our needs. God says, "Prove me (try me) . . ." (Malachi 3:10, AMP). The problem arises when giving becomes a type of con game to manipulate God to move on our behalf, rather than agreeing with and obeying the wholesome principles of His Word.

A believer isn't someone who simply pays tithes: a believer is a tither, and giving is a part of his lifestyle. But the man or woman who has a

42

get-rich-quick motivation views his tithes and offerings as some type of installment plan on God's biblical promises. Underneath is the intent to default on his side of the contract and run away with God's goods. This attitude always leans toward poverty. Although these people may experience some temporary financial success, it doesn't last because God isn't the focus of their motives. Deuteronomy 8:11–18 warns such defrauders as this:

> Beware that thou forget not the Lord thy God, in not keeping his commandments, and his judgments, and his statutes, which I command thee this day: Lest when thou hast eaten and art full, and hast built goodly houses, and dwelt therein; And when thy herds and thy flocks multiply, and thy silver and thy gold is multiplied and all that thou hast is multiplied; Then thine heart be lifted up, and thou forget the Lord thy God, which brought thee forth out of the land of Egypt, from the house of bondage; Who led thee through that great and terrible wilderness, wherein were fiery serpents, and scorpions, and drought, where there was no water; who brought thee forth water out of the rock of flint; Who fed thee in the wilderness with manna, which thy fathers knew not, that he might humble thee, and that he might prove thee, to do thee good at thy latter end; And thou say in thine heart My power and the might of mine hand hath gotten me this wealth. But thou shalt remember the Lord

thy God: For it is he that giveth thee power to get wealth, that he may establish his covenant which he sware unto thy fathers, as it is this day.

God's desire is to establish His covenant. He wants His people to use every financial resource to spread the "good news" around the world. When God's concerns become man's concerns, man breaks a strong link in the chain of poverty. And once a man can do that, he is on the way to true prosperity.

POVERTY SIGN # 5: NEGLECTING THE MATERIAL NEEDS OF THE WORK OF GOD

Thus speaketh the Lord of hosts, saying, This people say, The time is not come, the time that the Lord's house should be built. Then came the word of the Lord by Haggai the prophet, saying, Is it time for you, O ye, to dwell in your ceiled houses, and this house lie waste? Now therefore thus saith the Lord of hosts; Consider your ways. Ye have sown much, and bring in little; ye eat, but ye have not enough, ye drink, but ye are not filled with drink; ye clothe you, but there is none warm, and he that earneth wages earneth wages to put it into a bag with holes. Thus saith the Lord of hosts; Consider your ways. Go up to the mountain, and bring wood, and build the house; and I will take pleasure in it, and I will be glorified, saith the lord. Ye looked for much, and, lo, it came to little; and when ye brought it home, I did blow upon it. Why? saith the Lord of hosts. Because of mine house that is waste, and ye run every man unto his own house.

—HAGGAI 1:2–9

As Haggai prophesies in this passage, neglecting the material needs of the work of God leads to poverty. Malachi 3:10 (AMP) also says:

Bring all the tithes (the whole tenth of your income) into the storehouse, that there may be food in My house, and prove Me now by it, says the Lord of Hosts, if I will not open the windows of heaven for you and pour you out a blessing, that there shall not be room enough to receive it.

Another word for "food" in this Malachi verse is "resources." We are living in a society that uses money as a medium of exchange. But if the medium of exchange was eggs, then God would have eggs as a part of His "resources."

Resources are important because they make certain types of ministry go. For example, we know that the administrative part of our ministry is necessary, even if it's just to have enough money (resources) to print this book. Why? Because it is our intent to help those who read it to find God's truth for a better life.

In the day of the Old Testament, the temple or tabernacle was referred to as the House of God. Today, church buildings aren't the House of God;

they are only the home of the church. The church is people. Wherever people gather together it becomes their home. This is where responsibility comes in. We have a mission to build faith, hope, and love within the body of Christ, and to reflect the image of Jesus in the earth.

According to Haggai 1:8, God's people were told to go to the mountaintop and get the necessary materials. Then they were to come down and rebuild. Believers have received an abundance of revelation from the Word of God. They have been to the mountaintop. Because of this, they have a responsibility to take this mountaintop revelation to others.

How is this done? By giving to the gospel. We must give time, money, prayer, and work. By sowing in these areas we are building the house of God through building the church.

> Honour the Lord with thy substance, and
> with the firstfruits of all thine increase: So
> shall thy barns be filled with plenty, and
> thy presses shall burst out with new wine.
> —PROVERBS 3:9–10

By neglecting the spread of the gospel, we open the door to poverty and suppress the expansion of His kingdom on this earth.

POVERTY SIGN # 6: DISUNITY

Being a "loner" leads to poverty.

There is one alone, and there is not a
second; yea, he hath neither child nor
brother: yet is there no end of all his labour;
neither is his eye satisfied with riches; neither saith he, For whom do labour, and
bereave my soul of good? This is also
vanity, yea, it is a sore travail. Two are
better than one; because they have a good
reward for their labour. For if they fall, the
one will lift up his fellow: but woe to him
that is alone when he falleth; for he hath
not another to help him up. Again, if two lie
together, then they have heat: but how can
one be warm alone? And if one prevail
against him, two shall withstand him; and a
threefold cord is not quickly broken.
—ECCLESIASTES 4:8–12

This issue of separation has long been a
problem within American communities, especially black with white. Men haven't learned the
potential power that could be released from the
unity of races, cultures, and nations. There is
strength in unity.

Most of the major multi-billion-dollar conglom-
erates in America weren't built by one man. One
man may have had the idea, but it took several
men to make that idea work. When people with
ideas unite with people who have the skills to
make ideas work, the machinery is in place that
will pull people from the depths of poverty. This
can't be done by one man. It must be done
through unity.

We have learned this lesson at Abundant Life

Cathedral. We've learned that greater things can be done when we unite our time, resources, and finances. If we have a dollar we can't do very much with it. But if we are joined to a thousand people who each have one dollar, we can do a lot more. We can purchase more at a better price. We have bargaining power. The Scripture says, "A cord of three is better than one!" A person doesn't even have to be born again to understand this principle.

Hassles, arguments, tension, and stress can be avoided if men will first of all learn how to forgive one another and trust God. When we learn how to deal with people, we have won half the battle because unity paves the way to God's realm of prosperity. Disunity leads to poverty.

POVERTY SIGN # 7: LAZINESS

> He becometh poor that dealeth with a slack hand: but the hand of the diligent maketh rich. He that gathereth in summer is a wise son: but he that sleepeth in harvest is a son that causeth shame.
> —PROVERBS 10:4–5

Laziness is one of the prime causes of poverty. The apostle Paul tells us that a man who won't work to take care of his family is "worse than an infidel," an unbeliever (1 Tim. 5:8). An unbeliever doesn't place faith in the promises of God. Therefore, a man who doesn't add works to his faith is worse than a man who doesn't even acknowledge God or His Word.

In completing this chapter, I'm reminded of the farmer who prayed and fasted every day for God to give him a good crop. He would wake up at 9 A.M. each morning, pray until noon, and then go back to sleep. After about a month of this, he noticed that nothing was growing in his field. When he asked God about it, God replied, "Stop praying and plant the seeds I gave you."

A man can pray, fast, and mentally believe in God, but until he gets up and plants the seed (corresponding action) he will never get a crop. He must put action to his faith. Belief doesn't become living faith until it does something!

If men are to accomplish anything that is profitable, they are going to have to get up from that lazy seat, and start today! God doesn't expect individuals to complete a major project in one day, but He does expect them to start! The steering wheel of a car becomes useful only when the car is moving. It is much easier for God to maneuver and direct a moving target. So get up and move!

CHAPTER SIX

THE EFFECTS OF POVERTY IN BLACK AND WHITE

Within man is the natural desire to have his basic needs met. There is a sense of well-being when food, clothing, and shelter are provided. God recognized these basic needs in the Gospels when Jesus said, ". . . your Father knoweth what things ye have need of . . ." (Matt. 6:8). When these basic needs go unfulfilled people have a tendency to become frustrated and fearful. This is common in most low-income areas. In addition to this, many have placed themselves in deep debt just to help meet their

51

basic needs. Then the repayment of those debts becomes a need, and this adds pressure.

When people are unable to fulfill their basic needs, they begin to search for reasons why. This is one of the primary reasons the black community often seems at odds with what they call "white society." Slavery is recalled, hostilities are rekindled, and the cry for help goes out. Then when the cry for help is ignored, racial tension builds.

Many blacks blame whites for their economic situation, while many whites in this generation no longer feel a moral obligation to ease this inequality. This has been one of the primary causes of tension between the two races.

No man wants to feel less than any other human being, especially when this philosophy has already been inflicted upon one race of people by another. Although we know that poverty is a plight of all races, the percentage of poverty-stricken people is higher among blacks and hispanics in America. This spirit of poverty is carried over into the church. Today, a majority of predominantly black congregations struggle to pay rent and utilities costs, so world outreach ministry suffers.

Why? Well, "why" is a question that I believe can be answered through history. I recently learned that my great-great-grandfather was a preacher during the slave era. This discovery prompted me to do a little research. I found that preaching during the slave era carried powerful overtones of faith and hope. Although there was a great deal of suffering and injustice, these messages gave enslaved people hope for freedom, deliverance, and prosperity for the future. Faith was the primary element that enabled my black ancestors to endure the humiliation of slavery while at the same time allowed them to maintain some sense of dignity.

As time went on, much of the preaching and teaching began to center around the acceptance of suffering rather than the endurance of suffering. These concepts may seem related, but they are quite different. I'm sure you've heard many sermons and teachings on how we as Christians must be content to be sick, poor, or live in substandard conditions.

For some reason or other, men have linked holiness and relationship with God to a lifetime of suffering. Therefore, if we are to accept the will of God, such teaching holds, we must accept poverty and second-class citizenship in the human race. But this just isn't what the Bible teaches.

The Word of God doesn't teach us to accept suffering—it teaches us to endure suffering. When we endure suffering, we do so because we expect it to end at some point in the future.

That's why the apostle James wrote:

> Consider it wholly joyful, my brethren, whenever you are enveloped in or encounter trials of any sort or fall into various temptations. Be assured and understand that the trial and proving of your faith bring out endurance and steadfastness and patience. But let endurance and steadfastness and

patience have full play and do a thorough
work, so that you may be [people] perfectly
and fully developed [with no defects],
lacking in nothing.

—JAMES 1:2-4, AMP

When the Word of God says "lacking in
nothing" it means just that! Lack no-thing! No
man is poor until he accepts poverty within himself. I believe this is why Jesus said, "Take heed
what you hear." Romans 10:17 says, "Faith comes
by hearing, and hearing by the Word of God." So
if faith comes by hearing God's words (victorious
words), then fear and doubt come by hearing
Satan's words (defeated words).

For too long black people have been taught to
accept the circumstances of home evictions,
unemployment, debt, low incomes, job discrimi-
nation, and lack of education. So we must
remind everyone that these are not things to
accept, but things to endure and overcome! We
must see the end of our faith.

POVERTY DOCTRINE EFFECTS

When the forces of fear, doubt, and unbelief are
allowed into our personal lives, the church begins
to take on these attitudes. The church isn't a
building or organization; the church is people
who operate in a common idea of faith. But
because many in the church have accepted this
poverty doctrine, it has produced these results:

1. People aren't giving what they don't have.

2. People aren't giving what they fear they won't be able to replace.

3. People aren't receiving what they don't have the means to get.

So much of the church is suffering financially. And when the church suffers financially, the spreading of the gospel suffers.

Jesus said we are to preach the gospel (good news) to the poor. And again, the good news to the poor is that they don't have to be in bondage to poverty. The poor can be set free. They can get out of it! That's the good news the church must take to the masses of poor people. This is the good news that I believe will break the cycle of poverty. People must hear that message, trust God, and be set free from the cycle of debt. Then as people are set free from the grips of poverty, they are able to give financially to help spread the powerful message of prosperity to others.

God is very interested in every area of your life. It is His will that His creation experience prosperity—total prosperity! The apostle John wrote: "Beloved, I pray that you may prosper in every way and [that your body] may keep well, even as [I know] your soul keeps well and prospers" (3 John 2, AMP). For centuries people have been wishing good health and prosperity upon one another.

Jesus said:

> If ye then, being evil, know how to give
> good gifts unto your children, how much

more shall your Father which is in heaven
give good things to them that ask him?

—MATTHEW 7:11

So God wants men to experience overall prosperity. Again, when I speak of prosperity, many
people begin to see dollar signs! And, because we
understand the whole picture of prosperity now,
there is nothing wrong with that. God does desire
to prosper His people financially, just as He
wants people to prosper morally, physically, and
socially. And, contrary to what many may think,
all of these come from the spiritual realm. When
people are bound by social, moral and physical
poverty, it will ultimately show up in the financial area. This is why the apostle John wrote 3
John 2:

> Beloved, I pray that you may prosper in
> every way and [that your body] may keep
> well, even as [I know] your soul keeps well
> and prospers. . .(AMP).

Notice the Bible says, " . . . prosper in every
way [or in all things] . . . even as . . . your soul
prospers." There is a direct relationship between
the material (financial), physical, and spiritual
aspects of man. Therefore, whenever a man
chooses to come into relationship with God,
prosperity comes along with the package!
Poverty simply isn't a part of God's plan for our
lives!

If poverty was the way to God, Jesus would have
certainly said so, but He didn't. Instead, Jesus

spoke about the position we are to take. He tells us to give!

> Give, and [gifts] will be given to you, good measure, pressed down, shaken together, and running over, will they pour into [the pouch formed by] the bosom [of your robe and used as a bag].
>
> —LUKE 6:38, AMP

Throughout the New Testament we are encouraged, exhorted, and persuaded to give. The concept of giving is dealt with in Scripture from Genesis to Revelation.

Today, community service organizations raise funds for the needy. Giving is a display of love. Within the church, it is a display of love unto our Lord. But tell me, why would God expect people to give if they didn't have anything to give? He doesn't. That's right! It's God's will that people have, in order to give. The apostle Paul said:

> Let the thief steal no more, but rather let him be industrious, making an honest living with his own hands, so that he may be able to give to those in need.
>
> —EPHESIANS 4:28, AMP

Notice the phrase " . . . that he may be able...." God's will is that we have. We should not have just enough to meet our basic needs, but a surplus overflow that allows us to aid others. God didn't create us to be beggars; He created us to be suppliers!

CHAPTER SEVEN

GOD IS NOT
THE PROBLEM

The story is told about a six-year-old boy at his mother's funeral. As the boy sat through the funeral service with tears of grief streaming from his confused, tiny eyes, he heard the preacher, standing behind the coffin that held the remains of his mother, saying, "God has seen fit to take this woman home to heaven. The Lord giveth and the Lord taketh away."

I can imagine what was going through that young child's mind. He wasn't pondering the theological implications of looking for the love of

God between the lines. All he knew was that his mother, whom he loved, had left him alone. And now he was made to believe that somehow, God was responsible.

At some time in his later years, someone is going to tell this boy that God loves him. And even I would have a hard time believing that a God who would take my mother away when I needed her most really loved me. But the truth of the matter is: *God is not the problem.*

If we would take more time investigating the Bible, we would realize that God is not the problem. There is another being at work. His name is Satan! Jesus described him very accurately when He said, " . . . your father the devil . . . he is a liar, and the father of it. . . .The thief cometh not, but for to steal, and to kill, and to destroy: I am come that they might have life, and that they might have it more abundantly" (John 8:44; 10:10).

JOB: THE REAL STORY

I believe we need to clear up this misunderstanding about "the Lord giveth and the Lord taketh away" once and for all. And to do so, we must look at the Book of Job.

> And the Lord said to Satan, Have you considered My servant Job, that there is none like him on the earth, a blameless and upright man, one who [reverently] fears God and abstains from and shuns evil [because it is wrong]?
>
> Then Satan answered the Lord, Does Job

60

[reverently] fear God for nothing?

Have You not put a hedge about him and his house and all that he has, on every side? You have conferred prosperity and happiness upon him in the work of his hands, and his possessions have increased in the land.

But put forth Your hand now and touch all that he has, and he will curse You to Your face.

—Job 1:8–11, AMP

As we can see in this passage, Satan tried to get God to afflict Job. "But put forth Thine hand now, and touch all that he hath, and he shall curse Thee to Thy face." But God wouldn't do it! Let's go on a little further:

While he was yet speaking, there came also another and said, The fire of God (lightning) has fallen from the heavens and has burned up the sheep and the servants and consumed them, and I alone have escaped to tell you.

—Job 1:16, AMP

This fire didn't come from God. The servant attributed it to God since it came from the sky. But it originated with Satan. God wouldn't harm Job even though Job voiced his belief that God sent this destruction. So, as we can see from Job's concluding statements, what Job said throughout many portions of his book represented Job's belief—not what really happened.

> I had heard of You [only] by the hearing of
> the ear, but now my [spiritual] eye sees
> You. Therefore I loathe [my words] and
> abhor myself and repent in dust and ashes.
> —JOB 42:5–6, AMP

As we can see, Job eventually changed his mind about how God operated. Nevertheless, this belief about an angry God has been over-emphasized and perpetuated in the church over the years. Many believe God takes money from poor people to teach them how to be holy and righteous. This is a lie. Money has nothing to do with the absence or presence of holiness and righteousness. To believe that is to believe a lie of Satan.

Luke wrote of a woman who believed one of Satan's lies:

> And there was a woman there who for
> eighteen years had an infirmity caused by a
> spirit (a demon of sickness). She was bent
> completely forward and utterly unable to
> straighten herself up or to look upward.
> And when Jesus saw her, He called [her to
> Him] and said to her, Woman, you are
> released from your infirmity! Then He laid
> [His] hands on her and instantly she was
> made straight, and she recognized and
> thanked and praised God. But the leader of
> the synagogue, indignant because Jesus
> had healed on the Sabbath, said to the
> crowd, There are six days on which work
> ought to be done; so come on those days

and be cured, and not on the Sabbath day. But the Lord replied to him, saying, You playactors (hypocrites)! Does not each one of you on the Sabbath loose his ox or his donkey from the stall and lead it out to water it? And ought not this woman, a daughter of Abraham, whom Satan has kept bound for eighteen years, be loosed from this bond on the Sabbath day?

—Luke 13:11–16, AMP

This infirm woman was crippled to the point that she couldn't stand erect. And when Jesus diagnosed her problem, He said, ". . . whom Satan has kept bound . . . " Now stop and think for a moment: If God had put this woman in that position, do you really think His Son would undo His Father's work? Of course not. If He had, He would have been going against the will of His Father. And Jesus never went against the will of His Father.

On Earth As It Is in Heaven

When Jesus' disciples asked Him to teach them to pray, one of His statements was, "Thy will be done in earth as it is in heaven." Now let me ask you another question: Is there any sickness or poverty in heaven? No! And God wants his heavenly will to be performed in earth. So sickness and poverty is of Satan—not of God. Therefore, God is not your problem.

When people are brought to the realization that poverty is not some holy will of God, they are free to resist it and trust God for prosperity, which is His will.

The apostle Paul says:

> Let him who stole steal no longer, but rather let him labor, working with his hands what is good, that he may have something to give him who has need.
> —EPHESIANS 4:28, NKJV

Notice again the phrase " . . . that he may have something to give . . . " The gospel (good news) of Jesus Christ must be spread throughout the world. And since the world system is based on money, it takes money to spread the gospel.

When we realize that God is not against, but for prosperity, we begin to pray differently. We begin to approach God in the confidence that He is willing and eager to meet even our financial needs. This is why Jesus said over and over, "When you pray, believe that you receive."

The reason many of us never receive is because we doubt it is God's will. So believe that you receive! This is asking in faith! As Jesus said on many occasions, "Your faith has made you well!" God isn't against you; He is for you! Faith will make you whole. Faith will liberate you!

CHAPTER EIGHT

NO CURSE—
JUST BLESSING

Like most people, I've pondered the benefits of jobs and careers that promise to produce the greatest monetary gain. Everybody dreams at times about becoming a doctor, a lawyer, a professional athlete, or a recording artist. Young people daydream, wondering what it will be like after college or trade school. The dreams are great, the fantasy stimulating—but then comes reality. They don't become that doctor or lawyer. They find they can't even sing! Then they become frustrated and, eventually, complacent.

I have made a very interesting observation. It may not be very profound, but it is at least an observation. Prosperity doesn't begin with college, birthline, or whatever. Prosperity begins with knowing how God has dealt with poverty, and this knowledge will set people free.

> For ye know the grace of our Lord Jesus Christ, that, though he was rich, yet for your sakes he became poor, that ye through his poverty might be rich.
> —2 CORINTHIANS 8:9

Paul writes that Jesus, who was rich, became poor. Before He came to this earth, Jesus, the King of glory, was surrounded by the wealth of heaven. But the wealth of heaven isn't based on a monetary system. The gold and silver of heaven has no trade value because there is no buying or selling in heaven. Men place value based on what others consider valuable. But God isn't involved in the materialistic values of man. God is the Source of all providence. And since He is the Source, the wealth of heaven is merely a reflection of His own grandeur.

Now I didn't say that God doesn't consider anything valuable. On the contrary, He considers His creation valuable—especially man! John 3:16 tells us that "God so loved the world that He gave . . . " God exchanged the life of His own Son to provide man a way to enjoy fellowship with Him. Because of this ultimate gift, we can assume that man is of value to God.

Scripture is written in such a way that man

may understand it in relation to his own world. We can know from God's Word that Jesus left a life of "no limits" to identify with limited man. It's hard for man to understand this in human terms, so Paul paralleled this with an earthly concept: wealth. But when Jesus left the surroundings of heaven, He surely wasn't poor. How could He be? Jesus was the Creator of heaven and earth.

> For by him were all things created, that are in heaven, and that are in earth, visible and invisible, whether they be thrones, or dominions, or principalities, or powers: all things were created by him, and for him. And he is before all things, and by Him all things consist.
>
> —Colossians 1:16–17

So the phrase "he became poor" can't mean that Jesus became financially poor. Scripture reveals that Jesus and his disciples had a treasury. There were also supporters who financially contributed to His earthly ministry. (See Luke 8:2–3.) Many of the disciples had families, and Jesus certainly wouldn't leave the families of His disciples without a means of financial support while the disciples followed Him for three years. I personally believe the miracle of the "Great Fish Catch" in Luke 5 was used to provide their families with financial support while they were away.

When money for taxes was needed, the Bible tell us that Jesus told Peter to get the money out of the mouth of a fish. But Jesus also once told a listener:

The foxes have holes, and the birds of the
air have nests; but the Son of man hath not
where to lay his head.

—MATTHEW 8:20

This couldn't mean that Jesus had nowhere to
sleep. The Scriptures plainly tell us that Jesus fre-
quently visited the houses of friends and converts.
Jesus was merely pointing out to His would-be
followers the importance of priority and motivation.

So what is being said? Jesus became poor to
this world's system. In other words, Jesus didn't
look to earth's financial system as the source of
His supply. He came showing and teaching men
how to live independent of the world's financial
system. He taught men to live dependent on God
as their Source. Therefore, Matthew 8:20 deals
with living according to another source of
supply, another lifestyle. Paraphrasing James 2:5,
we find that: God has chosen the poor [bankrupt
to this world system] of this world to be rich
(wealthy through God's system).

FAITH UNLOCKS GOD'S SUPPLY

Living like this is entered into by faith, because
faith unlocks God's supply.

Mankind was redeemed from the curse of poverty to the blessings of God! But this redemption
means nothing if people don't use their dominion.
They must take their rightful possession.

To *take dominion* means "to tread down or to
rule in every area upon which your feet walk."

Man was created to be in control while under

God's control. Man was created to be prosperous in all areas. Notice in Genesis how God had made some fantastic provisions for Adam.

> And the Lord God planted a garden eastward in Eden; and there he put the man whom he had formed. And out of the ground made the Lord God to grow every tree that is pleasant to the sight, and good for food; the tree of life also in the midst of the garden, and the tree of knowledge of good and evil. And a river went out of Eden to water the garden; and from thence it was parted, and became into four heads. The name of the first is Pison: that is it which compasseth the whole land of Havilah, where there is gold.
>
> —Genesis 2:8–11

Adam was not to lack anything! Isn't that just like a father! Now, through Jesus Christ, the second Adam, we have received the same providence. The apostle Paul writes:

> For this one man, Adam, brought death to many through his sin. But this one man, Jesus Christ, brought forgiveness to many through God's mercy. Adam's one sin brought the penalty of death to many, while Christ freely takes away many sins and gives glorious life instead. The sin of this one man, Adam, caused death to be king over all, but all who will take God's gift of forgiveness and acquittal are kings of life

because of this one man, Jesus Christ.
—ROMANS 5:15–17, TLB

Can you see it? God's Word states that man has the channel in which to prosper in all ways! He is redeemed from the curse. I didn't say it! The Bible says it! Believers are redeemed from the curse of the law. Let me expand this thought through the use of an illustration that I gave in an earlier chapter: It is law that all cars stop when a traffic light turns red. If you violate that law and proceed through that traffic light, you run the risk of having an accident, crashing your car, getting a traffic ticket, or even losing your life.

So, the traffic law is good within itself. You wouldn't blame the city for the accident, would you? Of course not. It is designed to protect everybody. It only becomes an instrument of adversity when you violate its operation. So it is with spiritual law. The Law is good and beneficial to those who obey it. But it becomes man's instrument of poverty when its principles are violated.

> And it shall come to pass, if thou shalt hearken diligently unto the voice of the Lord thy God, to observe and to do all his commandments which I command thee this day, that the Lord thy God will set thee on high above all nations of the earth: And all these blessings shall come on thee, and overtake thee, if thou shalt hearken unto the voice of the Lord thy God. Blessed shalt thou be in the city, and blessed shalt thou be in the field. Blessed shall be the fruit of

thy body, and the fruit of thy ground, and
the fruit of thy cattle, the increase of thy
kine, and the flocks of thy sheep. Blessed
shall be thy basket and thy store. Blessed
shalt thou be when thou comest in and
blessed shalt thou be when thou goest out.

The Lord shall command the blessing
upon thee in thy storehouses, and in all that
thou settest thine hand unto; and He shall
bless thee in the land which the Lord thy
God giveth thee . . . And the Lord shall make
thee plenteous in goods, in the fruit of thy
body, and in the fruit of thy cattle, and in
the fruit of thy ground, in the land which
the Lord sware unto thy fathers to give thee.
The Lord shall open unto thee his good
treasure, the heaven to give the rain unto
thy land in his season, and to bless all the
work of thine hand: and thou shalt lend unto
many nations, and thou shalt not borrow.
And the Lord shall make thee the head, and
not the tail; and thou shalt be above only,
and thou shalt not be beneath; if that thou
hearken unto the commandments of the
Lord thy God, which I command thee this
day, to observe and to do them.

—Deuteronomy 28:1–6, 8, 11–13

Notice verse 12: "Thou shalt lend unto many
nations, and thou shalt not borrow."

But the negative side of this promise is found
in Deuteronomy 28:15–19, 38–44:

But it shall come to pass, if thou wilt not

71

hearken unto the voice of the Lord thy God, to observe to do all his commandments and his statues which I command thee this day; that all these curses shall come upon thee, and overtake thee. Cursed shalt thou be in the city, and cursed shalt thou be in the field. Cursed shall be thy basket and thy store. Cursed shall be the fruit of thy body, and the fruit of thy land, the increase of thy kine, and the flocks of thy sheep. Cursed shalt thou be when thou comest in, and cursed shalt thou be when thou goest out. . . . Thou shalt carry much seed out into the field, and shalt gather but little in; for the locust shall consume it. Thou shalt plant vineyards, and dress them, but shalt neither drink of the wine, nor gather the grapes; for the worms shall eat them. Thou shalt have olive trees throughout all thy coasts, but thou shalt not anoint thyself with the oil; for thine olive shall cast his fruit. Thou shalt beget sons and daughters, but thou shalt not enjoy them, for they shall go into captivity. All thy trees and fruit of thy land shall the locust consume. The stranger that is within thee shall get up above thee very high; and thou shalt come down very low. He shall lend to thee, and thou shalt not lend to him: he shall be the head, and thou shalt be the tail.

CHRISTIANITY IS IMPOSSIBLE OUTSIDE OF CHRIST

Without Jesus Christ living His life through us,

believers can't possibly keep God's law. Without Him, the ability simply isn't there. To turn away from God leaves finances in an accursed state.

> Even from the days of your fathers ye are gone from mine ordinances, and have not kept them. Return unto me, and I will return unto you, saith the Lord of hosts. But ye said, Wherein shall we return? Will a man rob God ? Yet ye have robbed me. But ye say, Wherein have we robbed thee? In tithes and offerings. Ye are cursed with a curse: for ye have robbed me, even this whole nation.
> —MALACHI 3:7–9

CURED OF THE CURSE

The apostle Paul provided us with tremendous biblical insight relating to the reversal of the curse through Jesus Christ when he wrote:

> Christ hath redeemed us from the curse of the law, being made a curse for us: for it is written, Cursed is everyone that hangeth on a tree.
> —GALATIANS 3:13

What was the tree? It was the cross of Calvary. When Jesus was nailed to the cross at Calvary, He became the essence of the curse itself! He literally took the curse of the law (penalty of violating the law) in His own body. We know that the curse included sin, sickness, disease, eternal punishment, and a multitude of other things. But the Deuteronomy curse also spoke of poverty. So Jesus also took poverty. Hallelujah! The principles that promote it died on Calvary with Him!

Why did Jesus do it? What would be the benefits?

> That the blessing of Abraham might come on the Gentiles through Jesus Christ; that we might receive the promise of the Spirit through faith.
>
> —GALATIANS 3:14

What is the "blessing (prosperous state) of Abraham"?

> And I will make of thee a great nation, and I will bless thee, and make thy name great; and thou shalt be a blessing: And I will bless them that bless thee, and curse him that curseth thee: 'and in thee shall all families of the earth be blessed.
>
> —GENESIS 12:2–3

> And I will make thee exceeding fruitful, and I will make nations of thee, and kings shall come out of thee. And I will establish my covenant between me and thee and thy seed after thee in their generations for an everlasting covenant, to be a God unto thee, and to thy seed after thee.
>
> —GENESIS 17:6–7

What is a Gentile? A Gentile is a non-Jew, or one considered to be alienated from the covenant. And one of Abraham's promises was that nations (plural), meaning others, would come from him. Therefore, entrance into prosperity is not based upon race, but upon the act of Jesus. This is important. Prosperity is not connected to the color of one's skin, but to the power and love of God! Praise God!

When Jesus Christ is received as Lord and Savior, a man becomes His child—an offspring of God! And the Word says:

> For ye are all the children of God by faith in Christ Jesus. For as many of you as have been baptized into Christ have put on Christ.
> —GALATIANS 3:26–27

To put Christ on is to receive Him and all He has to give. It is to identify with Him, His death, burial and resurrection, and all that comes with and proceeds from Him! Notice that verse 28 says:

> There is neither Jew nor Greek, there is neither bond nor free, there is neither male nor female: for ye are all one in Christ Jesus.

What Christ has given is not based on gender, lineage or material possessions, but on who we belong to and with whom we identify.

Through Jesus Christ something wonderful has taken place.

And if ye be Christ's, then are ye Abraham's
seed, and heirs according to the promise.
—v. 29

Through Christ, man possesses all that God
promised to Abraham! He is Abraham's spiritual
seed! He is Abraham's heir! (In position for an
inheritance!) And that inheritance, among many
other things, includes financial prosperity.

Promises, Promises, Promises, Promises

God has provided us with so many promises.
Here are only a few of the many thousands that
emphasize His biblical will of prosperity. Look at
them! Hear them! Feed on them! They are life!

Only be thou strong and very courageous,
that thou mayest observe to do according
to all the law, which Moses my servant
commanded thee: turn not from it to the
right hand or to the left, that thou mayest
prosper withersoever thou goest. This book
of the law shall not depart out of thy
mouth; but thou shalt meditate therein day
and night, that thou mayest observe to do
according to all that is written therein: for
then thou shalt make thy way *prosperous*,
and then thou shalt have good success.
—Joshua 1:7–8

Let them shout for joy, and be glad, that
favour my righteous cause: yea, let them say
continually, Let the Lord be magnified, which

hath pleasure in the *prosperity* of his servant.
—PSALM 35:27, EMPHASIS ADDED

And he shall be like a tree planted by the rivers of water, that bringeth forth his fruit in his season; his leaf also shall not wither; and whatsoever he doeth shall *prosper.*
—PSALM 1:3, EMPHASIS ADDED

Then answered I them, and said unto them, The God of heaven, he will *prosper* us; therefore we his servants will arise and build: but ye have no portion, nor right, nor memorial, in Jerusalem.
—NEHEMIAH 2:20, EMPHASIS ADDED

And the elders of the Jews builded, and they *prospered* through the prophesying of Haggai the prophet and Zechariah the son of Iddo. And they builded, and finished it, according to the commandment of the God of Israel, and according to the command-ment of Cyrus, and Darius, and Artaxerxes, king of Persia.
—EZRA 6:14, EMPHASIS ADDED

And they rose early in the morning, and went forth into the wilderness of Tekoa: and as they went forth, Jehoshaphat stood and said, Hear me, O Judah, and ye inhabi-tants of Jerusalem; Believe in the Lord your God, so shall ye be established; believe His prophets, so shall ye *prosper.*
—2 CHRONICLES 20:20, EMPHASIS ADDED

Where is the wise? where is the scribe?
where is the disputer of this world? hath not
God made foolish the wisdom of this world?
—1 CORINTHIANS 1:20

But my God shall supply all your need according to His riches in glory by Christ Jesus.
—PHILIPPIANS 4:19

Beloved, I wish above all things that thou
mayest prosper and be in health, even as
thy soul prospereth.
—3 JOHN 2

God has given these promises of prosperity
through Jesus Christ. He has given them, but we
must receive them; and they must be taught!

CHAPTER NINE

THE UNSEEN
FORCE

Poverty is the offspring of fear, and fear is rampant in the lives of many today. There is the fear of not having enough, the fear of rejection, the fear of being inadequate, the fear of being unqualified, and the fear of not having security in the future. When a man is bound by fear, all his creative energies are stifled because fear counters productivity.

There aren't many incidences in Scripture where God wasn't dealing in some way or another with the fears of men. Jesus often told His followers to

"Fear not." Fear is a faith crippler. So as long as there is fear in a person's life, God can't move on their behalf. God is not a God who responds to fear. He responds to faith, and faith, is an unseen force.

> Now faith is the substance of things hoped
> for, the evidence of things not seen.
> —HEBREWS 11:1

At one time, I believed that if I had some extra money, I would really have it made as far as building a congregation. I had it all planned. I would buy some radio and television time, print some flyers, and rent a building. I daydreamed about this often. But as time passed, I came to the conclusion that the money wasn't coming (at least not that way). It was then that I knew I would have to start with what I had. The only problem was I didn't think I had anything to start with! I was even afraid of losing the little I had. So I waited and wondered where and how I could start with nothing.

I searched for a clue in Scripture and finally realized from Hebrews 11:1 that faith was the beginning. Then I decided to start believing that something could be done. My only starting substance was faith.

Faith? Yes, faith! I noticed the words "substance." I could begin with "the substance of things hoped for . . ." and faith was that substance.

Let's remember the account of the woman who had a disease that caused her to hemorrhage in Mark 5:

Now a certain woman had a flow of blood
for twelve years, and had suffered many
things from many physicians. She had spent
all that she had and was no better, but
rather grew worse. When she heard about
Jesus, she came behind Him in the crowd
and touched His garment; for she said, "If
only I may touch His clothes, I shall be
made well." Immediately the fountain of her
blood was dried up, and she felt in her
body that she was healed of the affliction.

—MARK 5:25–29, NKJV

Notice verse 26 in this passage: She had spent
all that she had and was no better, but rather
grew worse. This woman was at the bottom of
her barrel. No hopes, no dreams, and now no
money! On top of that, she was getting worse!
She had no substance. What happened to her?
Verse 27 says, "When she heard about Jesus . . . "
This was the beginning of her faith.

Faith cometh by hearing, and hearing by
the word of God.

—ROMANS 10:17

When the woman heard about Jesus' works,
words, and miracles she had hope, but hope
wasn't enough. According to verse 28, she started
saying what she was believing: "If only I may
touch His clothes, I shall be made well." Faith
was now coming alive inside of her! Then, she
acted on her faith by going to Jesus.

Jesus clearly honored and answered this

woman's faith in verse 34:

> Daughter, your faith has made you well. Go
> in peace, and be healed of your affliction.

What made her well? Her faith. Although she had spent all she had, faith became her substance.

The greatest excuse that can be given when facing any need is that there isn't anything to start with, but there is! There is faith! Faith will always get the attention of God. It is how God operates.

UNDERSTANDING THE FAITH FORCE

> ...and with all thy getting get under-
> standing.
>
> —PROVERBS 4:7

Wisdom is the key to understanding faith. You can sit in an automobile all day, but unless the key is put in the ignition and turned, you will never operate the car. Putting the key in an ignition is a simple task. But suppose you had never seen a car. Suppose you had never even heard of a car. If this was the case, you would have great difficulty putting the key in a car's ignition because you wouldn't understand how an automobile works.

The same is true when we deal with the things of God. There are many potential sources of prosperity around us, but how do they work? How will they benefit people? There is a lack of understanding concerning how things work, and this understanding only comes by faith.

> By faith we understand that the worlds
> were framed by the word of God, so that
> the things which are seen were not made of
> things which are visible.
>
> —HEBREWS 11:3, NKJV

The invisible world of God's Spirit is seen through the eyes of faith. Faith enables men to see past poverty and lay hold of prosperity—through God's promises. Prosperity is "out there" in the realm of those things that aren't visible, but the substance of faith will lay hold of them for use.

BEGINNING TO USE THE UNSEEN FORCE

Suppose I made an appointment to meet with you Saturday at noon to give you a car. If you knew me as a man of my word, there would be no reason to miss our appointment—especially if I promised to give you a car! (You would probably be there two hours early!) Your receiving the car would depend on the faith you placed in my word to meet you at noon.

It's the same with God's promises. God is a Person of His word. If He says something, He means it! If He says He will richly provide for you, you can take Him at His Word.

What was Jesus' reply to Satan in Matthew 4 when he tempted Him to turn stones into bread?

> It is written, Man shall not live by bread
> alone, but by every word that proceedeth
> out of the mouth of God.

The Word of God is bread for daily life. We live by the Word of God because God's Word is life. God has given over seven thousand promises that He intends to keep. But promises mean nothing unless someone acts on them through faith. Too many want God to surprise them with a "free car" out of nowhere, because, you know, "He's good!" And God is good! But faith will enter a covenant relationship with God that will inspire the kind of corresponding actions the woman with the issue of blood experienced. Faith hears, speaks, *and* acts. There is substance in this, and God will bless it.

> Blessed be the God and Father of our Lord Jesus Christ, who hath blessed us with all spiritual blessings in heavenly places in Christ.
>
> —EPHESIANS 1:2

God is committed to His children's prosperity—in every area of life. The unseen force of faith will powerfully release it.

CHAPTER TEN

THE POWER
TO PERFORM

How many times have you had an idea, but never proceeded any further with it? Probably many times. Maybe you even forgot about it—only to be reminded of it when someone else publicly unveiled it and made millions of dollars! Then you said, "Why didn't I do that when I had the chance?" That's the question! Why?

God is the Author of all creative acts. Genesis 1:1–2 says:

In the beginning God (prepared, formed, fashioned, and) created the heavens and the earth.

The earth was without form and an empty waste, and darkness was upon the face of the very great deep. The Spirit of God was moving (hovering, brooding) over the face of the waters (AMP).

From this point, God began to create the principle elements of this earth through His spoken Word. This creation came forth out of the midst of chaos and confusion. Along with the chaos and confusion, there was "the Spirit of God moving upon the face of the waters" (Gen. 1:2). So the creative power was there all the time. But it wasn't until God said, "Let there be light" (Gen. 1:3) that the potential creative power began to perform the act of creation.

It is possible to have the power to be creative, but still not actually create. This, I believe, is what is holding many in the chains of poverty. They have the creative ideas, but they don't know how to bring them into physical reality.

That's right! If we are believers, we have the creative power of God within us. The apostle John wrote that the Creator Himself abides within us:

Ye are of God, little children, and have overcome them: because greater is he that is in you, than he that is in the world.

—1 JOHN 4:4

The apostle Paul wrote:

And [so that you can know and understand]
what is the immeasurable and unlimited
and surpassing greatness of His power in
and for us who believe, as demonstrated in
the working of His mighty strength, Which
He exerted in Christ when He raised Him
from the dead and seated Him at His [own]
right hand in the heavenly [places].
—Ephesians 1:19–20, amp

The creative power of God is within you. God
put it there! Of course, man doesn't have the ultimate creative power which is resident in God. We
only have that power in limited measure. But it is
there!

Writing to his young protégé, Paul told Timothy,
to "guard . . . the deposit . . . " (1 Tim. 6:20).

Jesus explained the creative potential of those
in His kingdom this way:

The kingdom of heaven is like to a grain of
mustard seed, which a man took, and
sowed in his field.
—Matthew 13:31

We know that the seed is the Word, and that
the soil (ground) is the heart (innermost being) of
man. So Jesus said, in essence, that if a man takes
the Word (the deposit) and plants it within himself, it's going to develop and expand!

Hebrews 12:9 tells us that God is the Father of
spirits. This is where God works—through the
spirit of man. When the spirit of man is pregnant
with the creative force of God (the Word), the

spirit will ultimately give birth.

Jesus also typed the Word of God with leaven:

> The kingdom of heaven is like unto leaven,
> which a woman took and hid in three mea-
> sures of meal, till the whole was leavened.
> —Matthew 13:33

In this parable, Jesus showed that the leaven caused an expansion of the elements. And He explained that the creativity of God in the believer is like this. It expands to permeate the things beyond its place of origin. Let me give you an example.

During the first year of the founding of our church, I worked as a computer-supply salesman. I was doing the best I could in sales. But even if I sold more, I couldn't receive the commissions fast enough to pay the outstanding bills. And my family was going through a financial challenge, so we needed some extra money.

Then one day while I was on the phone with a customer, the remark was made that we didn't have a brochure. My customer said that if she had known we sold certain items, she would have bought them from us. So she made me realize that we were losing money because of a lack of information. I went to my employer and relayed the need, but he said it would cost him hundreds of dollars just to call in an advertising layout man.

BE AVAILABLE, AND WILLING TO WORK

Well, for years I had done the artwork and layout

for our ministry brochures and ads. So to meet this need, I volunteered to do the same work, but at a third of the cost! That meant long hours of overtime, but I was willing to pay the price. My employer accepted my offer, I produced the layout, and within seven days I received the money needed to pay our bills!

I must admit this was hard work and caused some sleepless nights. But it all started from a creative idea! I believe this idea came as a result of the Word of God inside of me because the Word produces an attitude of giving. Luke 6:38 says:

> Give, and it shall be given unto you; good measure, pressed down, and shaken together, and running over, shall men give into your bosom. For with the same measure that ye mete withal it shall be measured to you again.

Why don't we capitalize on our ideas and bring them into physical reality?

I believe the apostle Paul sheds some light on this:

> For I know that nothing good dwells within me, (that is, in my flesh). I can will what is right, but I cannot perform it [I have the intention and urge to do what is right, but no power to carry it out.]
>
> —ROMANS 7:18, AMP

The word *perform* in this Amplified Bible passage comes from a Greek word meaning "to accomplish." In other words, to perform is to accomplish what we will or desire to do! And it is in between these two areas—the creative idea and the accomplishing of that idea—that poverty first plants its seeds.

Jesus related this truth in His parable of the tares:

> The kingdom of heaven is likened unto a man which sowed good seed in his field: But while men slept, his enemy came and sowed tares among the wheat, and went his way. But when the blade was sprung up, and brought forth fruit, then appeared the tares also.
>
> —MATTHEW 13:24–26

REFUSE SATAN'S CROP!

Isn't it ironic that just when fruit is about to be produced, circumstances come to hinder the harvest? The weeds in this parable appear during the time when the seed is producing fruit. Jesus said this was going to happen. So even though God fills His believers with the creative power of His Word, Satan is there tromping through God's field scattering his seeds of doubt, laziness, procrastination, inferiority, social stigma, and confusion. But if I know this, I can make a determination to "push forward" in spite of these things. I can recognize Satan's crop and refuse to harvest it.

I will be the first to admit that recognizing and rejecting Satan's crop is easier said than done, but a tare is a tare and wheat is wheat! And once we understand the process, we can guard our crop. Then we can help others guard theirs by continually encouraging them in God's truth. Like the apostle Paul, we can help them press upward to harvest God's promises of well-being in life.

> I press toward the mark for the prize of the high calling of God in Christ Jesus.
> —PHILIPPIANS 3:14

Notice the word "press" Paul uses in this verse. Its use indicates a pushing, a straining of all that is within us. We must tell men that to merely quote and claim scriptures, and to even pray one hour—then sit back—is not enough! We must tell them that there will be difficult times and that they must arm themselves with the promises of God's Word which will assure them of success when confronted by life's problems.

THE POWER TO PERFORM

If Satan can stop believers when their seed is merely planted in the field, they will never get close to harvest. They will never realize what God could have done with their idea. This, I believe, is where God intends us to exercise the *force of faith* which produces *the power to perform*. This power counteracts satanic power. Many within black and impoverished communities have allowed poverty to begin breeding at this point.

The *power to perform* is a must if we are to transform creative ideas into physical realities. No matter how many ideas we have or how much education (know-how) we possess, if faith isn't present, we can live our entire lives without accomplishing anything.

I'll never forget when Sandra and I decided to get out of debt. Abundant Life Cathedral was a young church and couldn't support us financially. As I mentioned, I was an office supply salesman and Sandra worked in a daycare center. We would anticipate our upcoming paychecks, knowing they wouldn't provide enough to cover our present bills—let alone get out of debt!

We continued to pray, tithe, and give offerings, and God gave us the wisdom to manage our money. To our natural eye it looked as if there was no hope. It looked as if we would never catch up. But we finally came to the place of seeing with our eyes of faith! The substance of faith became our *power to perform*. And the *power to perform* gave us the energy to search for creative ways to get out of debt, hear the voice of God, and to get into the flow of what God wanted to do! I will share some of this wisdom in chapter 11, but it will be up to you to mix it with faith. (See Hebrews 4:2.)

Faith will get you through the pressures of the enemy. Satan is a liar, but a lie has short legs and will ultimately run out. God's Word is truth, and truth will endure throughout the passage of time. So hang your faith on God's Word. Your faith will liberate you!

CHAPTER ELEVEN

BREAKING THE SPIRIT OF POVERTY

If the spirit of poverty has been oppressing your life, the poverty cycle must be broken. I don't like to give formulas because all formulas don't work for all people. Every person has a different set of values and the conditions for receiving promises can vary with each individual. But there are some basic scriptural steps that everyone can use to walk out of poverty. So I submit them now for your consideration.

Step 1—Put Poverty in Its Rightful Position

First of all, you need to know that Jesus gave you something of inestimable value to empower you for a prosperous life.

> In my name shall they cast out devils . . .
> they shall lay hands on the sick and they
> shall recover.
>   —Mark 16:17

Jesus gave us His name to destroy the works of Satan and overcome in life. This doesn't mean that using the name of Jesus will work as a magical word. On the contrary, when we use His name, we use His authority. Jesus has given us authority, but we must use it!

People are too often persuaded that they have no choices in life. It seems to many as if God has left them on this planet to fall victim to the vicious forces of this world's system. Religion has even taught us this. We have preached a message of "maybe and maybe not." But God is a God of specifics. He is specific about His Word, about the believers' life, and about His care for them.

I remember a boy named Arthur from elementary school who was a real bully. Everyone was afraid of Arthur—myself included. This boy was so threatening that I would hide behind trees or cross over to the other side of the street just to avoid him. But over a period of time this became very inconvenient. So I finally decided to put a stop to it.

I was determined to face Arthur the next time

our paths crossed. And when they did, we had a fight. To this day I'm not sure who won that fight, but from that moment on I never let the presence of Arthur dictate the course of my life. I never crossed another street that I didn't want to cross or delay myself by hiding behind a tree.

This is what authority does. When people recognize that the devil has been defeated, they no longer hide from him or the areas he has affected. When people discover their authority in Jesus' name, they no longer hide from creditors or feel ashamed of their present occupations. They realize that regardless of what their bank account says, the Word says they're more than a conqueror. They are then encouraged to stop running and hiding.

It is here that the believer must trust the power of God to manifest itself in the sphere of conquering. Conquering what? Conquering the physical and spiritual results of poverty. There will be a learning curve, and conflict here. When a person chooses to change habits that have been forged over the years, there will always be an initial conflict.

I remember the first church I pastored. I had a wife, a daughter, and a son on the way. We had no medical insurance or any other source of income. On top of that, my starting salary was $90 a week! That's right, a whopping $90 a week! Yet, even with such a low income, I was approved for credit cards! I was approved to go in debt. So we used those cards to finance a baby bed, diapers, milk, clothes, and many other things that we needed. And before long, we formed a habit of depending upon plastic. Over the years, this habit almost ruined us financially. Did I say almost? Well, it did ruin us! It took us several years to get out of credit card debt and to clear our names on various credit reports. For years that credit report followed us like a hound dog chasing a raccoon!

We eventually cleared everything up and started again. But I'll never forget that day when we first experienced the conquering power of Jesus Christ. It was on that day when Sandra and I sat down, took authority over our spending habits, fought the urge to use credit, and cut up our charge cards! Yes, we cut them up!

Now, I must be honest with you. I'm not a cut-up-all-the-credit-cards-and-never-use-one-for-the-rest-of-your-life fanatic. As a matter of fact, I have one now. But we never charge more than we are able to pay off each month. My point is, at the time we took our "cutting" action, the financial lifestyle we were living exceeded our ability to pay for it. We had formed some bad habits, and those habits had to be broken. Drastic circumstances demanded drastic measures.

Our problem wasn't the credit cards—the problem was us! So we had to face up to our problem, admit our mistake, and turn from the direction in which we were headed.

What are some of the things that control people and keep them in poverty? Is it credit cards? An overextended lifestyle? A drive to live out financial fantasies? Habitual borrowing? Slothfulness in paying bills? Whatever is in control, the Word of God demands that believers break free. And you do this by totally committing to the truth of Jesus Christ.

> For whosoever will lose his life for my sake shall find it.
> —MATTHEW 16:25

God knows the needs of His people, and He promises to provide for them. But His promises are contingent upon our complete abandonment unto Him.

> But seek ye first [or aim at] the kingdom of God, and his righteousness, and all these things shall be added unto you.
> —MATTHEW 6:33

So, as I encourage families and individuals to look at their lifestyles and to make any necessary changes, I expect to see great financial progress. I teach God's people to stand tall, fight, and declare: "Finances, debt, poverty, habits—I take my stand against you and refuse to let you take a stand against me in Jesus' name! Jesus has given me victory over you, so go in Jesus' name!" This is where I teach people to start. I teach that poverty has a rightful position—right out of the lives of the people of God!

STEP 2—ACKNOWLEDGE THE SOURCE THROUGH GIVING

Like some of you, I grew up in the church, and vividly remember the atmosphere of the worship service during the offering. It was as if God had taken a fifteen-minute recess and walked out of the service! We must be reminded that giving is one of God's steps out of poverty.

Malachi 3:7 says:

> Even from the days of your fathers ye are gone away from mine ordinances, and have not kept them. Return unto me, and I will return unto you, saith the Lord of hosts. But ye said, Wherein shall we return?

Malachi is describing the futile reality of a people who have walked away from God. He is addressing people who have rejected God's declared lifestyle. This was the reason for Israel's poverty. So God was saying, "Return to me. . ." And how were they to return? Through giving, because verse 8 says:

> Will a man rob God? Yet ye have robbed me.
> But ye say, Wherein have we robbed thee?
> In tithes and offerings.

Israel was guilty of robbing God, so the reinstitution of the system of tithes and offerings was the only way back. What? Tithes and offerings get us back to God? Yes, as far as national and individual prosperity are concerned.

Remember Deuteronomy 8:18:

> But thou shalt remember the Lord thy God: for it is he that giveth thee power to get wealth. . .

Now notice the word *power.* It comes from the Hebrew word meaning "ability." So ability to make money comes from God! Therefore, to deny God first access to finances is to place other things in front of Him.

The tithe and offering are to come out of our income first! From the top! This giving from the top acknowledges God as Lord of our finances.

Proverbs 3:9 says:

> Honor the Lord with thy substance, and with the firstfruits of all thine increase.

When this is done, we walk under the system of blessing—not cursing.

> Ye are cursed with a curse: for ye have robbed me, even this whole nation. Bring ye all the tithes into the storehouse, that there may be meat in mine house, and prove me now herewith, saith the Lord of hosts, if I will not open you the windows of heaven, and pour you out a blessing, that there shall not be room enough to receive it.
>
> —MALACHI 3:9–10

But now you ask, "What if I can't afford to tithe?" To answer this, let me remind you that God taught Israel about giving in the midst of their poverty—so you can't afford not to tithe! You must have strength, ideas, ability, and energy to make money, and these come from God. So to withhold God's tithe, to rob from Him, is to bite the hand that feeds you. God is not against you;

He is for you! But you must absolutely and enthusiastically return to the principle of the tithe and offering to break free from the spirit of poverty and debt.

There has been a great outcry over the past number of years regarding the financial resources of religious organizations. And this has resulted in many church leaders and pastors equivocating on the subject of tithes and offerings.

I remember being challenged by one of the men in our congregation. "Pastor, do you believe that tithes and offerings are the way through which God provides for His people?" he asked.

I responded by saying, "Yes, I do."

So he said, "Do you really believe that?"

To this I replied, "Yes, I really do!"

Then he said something to me that I have never forgotten: "Then never be ashamed to teach it with assurance."

This is what church leaders and believers must avidly and unequivocally do. We must teach one another God's method of financial release with assurance.

I have related some principles, concepts, and ideas throughout this book that I believe will cause people to climb out of poverty—if they will apply them. Many of these teachings can even be used by the business community to make a lot of money. But along with financial prosperity comes the temptation to fall in love with financial success. The possibility of loving money is always there. This is why the apostle Paul says:

> The love of money is the root of all evil. . .
> —1 TIMOTHY 6:10

Notice that Paul said, the love of money—not money in and of itself—but the love of money is the root of all evil. This is where I believe the tithe comes in. As long as God's people acknowledge God through the tithe; no matter how much money is made, the attitude will always be one of dependence on God.

Many have been confused about this. Some divide the tithe and spread it out among different ministries, family members or various charities. But the Word is very specific: "Bring ye all the tithes into the storehouse." The storehouse is where the resources of God are kept. Where is the gathering of God's resources? The church, or the body of Christ on earth.

Are you in a local church? Is that church growing in faith and love? Are you receiving revelation from the Word of God through your church? Is your spirit being fed? Are you growing in ability, faith, and energy? Then give your tithe to the church where you are planted. What has helped you grow must continue to grow. And your tithes and offerings along with those of others in your local body will help the ministry expand and bless others.

God promised those who give tithes and offerings that He would: ". . . open you the windows of heaven, and pour you out a blessing, that there shall not be room enough to receive it." So again, you can't afford not to give.

For years I thought the windows of heaven

were somewhere in the sky. Then I slowly discovered that wherever Jesus is, you'll find the windows of heaven! God doesn't drop money out of the sky! He pours it out of the "windows of heaven." In other words, He infuses you with power, ideas, energy, and ability! Out of you comes the potential to get wealth. It's in you! Praise God!

STEP 3—PUT FEET TO YOUR FAITH

Let me explain something very interesting about money. Money is acquired through ideas, ability, and the exchange of work and energy. For example, if you work for a company at the rate of $5 an hour, eight hours a day, your income for one day will be $40. Now that $40 equals the amount of ideas, ability, and work, you exchange for one day.

Ideas x Ability x Work = Money

Now I'm going to say something that gets right to the heart of breaking the poverty spirit. I have been stressing throughout this book the concepts of ideas and ability. These are the things that God puts inside of the believer. Even the unbeliever has this dynamic duo. But what causes these two powerful forces to activate is work. Yes, work! People must put feet to their faith. They must be encouraged to convert ideas and ability into action!

One of the greatest deceptions that has caused many people to become frustrated and to give up hope is the belief that their future depends on a job. Let me stress the importance of not merely looking for a job—but learning to look for work! There is a difference. Most people limit seeking a job to their particular field; or to their line of experience; or to a certain salary; or to their sphere of education. If they don't find a job in any of these four categories they give up and wind up in the unemployment line.

But work is anything that will yield a harvest—regardless of whether it meets a person's certain qualifications or not. Work isn't limited to a certain field of endeavor. It is just what it says—work!

Many times, people will have to take a lower-paying position in order to temporarily make ends meet, and God will honor this.

Take, for example, Ruth:

> And Ruth the Moabitess said unto Naomi, Let me now go to the field, and glean ears of corn after him in whose sight I shall find grace. And she said unto her, Go, my daughter. And she went, and came, and gleaned in the field after the reapers: and her hap was to light on a part of the field belonging unto Boaz, who was of the kindred of Elimelech.
>
> —RUTH 2:2–3

Ruth was unskilled, inexperienced, and unemployed. But if she was going to survive, she knew she had to work. The first job she took was gleaning. As a matter of fact, gleaning was the system that God provided to care for the poor and unemployed.

And when ye reap the harvest of your land,
thou shalt not wholly reap the corners of
thy field, neither shalt thou gather the
gleanings of thy harvest. And thou shalt not
glean thy vineyard, neither shalt thou
gather every grape of thy vineyard; thou
shalt leave them for the poor and stranger: I
am the Lord your God.

—Leviticus 19:9–10

This is the way the system worked: When
landowners reaped their harvest, they were for-
bidden to pick up the grain their harvesters left
behind. It was to be left for the poor. What is sig-
nificant to note here is that God didn't command
the landowners to harvest all their crops and give
a handout to the poor. No, He provided a system
where the poor could work that allowed them to
experience the dignity and honor that comes
from good, honest labor. Gleaning was back-
breaking work. But, if a person stuck to it, he or
she could yield a minimum living. That was
God's welfare system. The people had to work
for it.

So if you're struggling with a spirit of poverty,
let me encourage you to wake up, get up, stand
up, dress up—and move out into the work force.
Let me exhort you to break out of a workless attitude, if that happens to be your case. Get up
early tomorrow morning, wash your face, comb
your hair, put on clean clothes, and go out
trusting God to find work—work of any sort—
until it leads to God's best.

I believe churches should consider providing

certain chores and paying individuals for good honest work rather than supplying people from a benevolence fund. Of course there will be some situations that are exceptions, but the job of church leadership is more than to feed the belly. We must feed the spirit and the attitude of displaced people.

Men don't work to make money—money is a result of their work. And work is a stimulus to the dignity of the human being. God knew this. That's why God put Adam in the garden and put him to work. Adam was commanded to "keep" the garden or to "cultivate" it. So from the beginning of time, there has been a satisfaction to be gained from working with one's hands and seeing the fruit of one's labor.

Work was not a part of the Genesis 3 curse. But working independently of a relationship to the Creator will produce little fruit and few, if any, rewards. This is the curse. Work without ideas and ability produces little. But when a man works with the creativity and ability of God flowing through him, the true meaning of work is put in its proper, relational perspective. This I believe is the will of God: to work in relationship with our Creator. Are you beginning to see the connection?

When we give, we aren't just giving money; we're giving a portion of our time, ability, ideas, and energy. And since people exchange money for food, clothing, shelter, and the necessities of life, when they give, they're giving a portion of their lives. This is an important point. Money is a part of life.

STEP 4—LOOK BEYOND YOUR PRESENT CIRCUMSTANCES

There was a point in our lives when Sandra and I couldn't see past poverty. We were surrounded by reminders of how poor we were. We grew up looking at run-down neighborhoods, riding in old used cars, suffering unemployment because of the economy or racism, and in the middle of all this, listening to religious teachings that God wanted to make and keep you poor in order to relate to you. Can you imagine what kind of image we carried around within us? Not very encouraging, I guarantee you. If that's the kind of picture a person is constantly receiving, that's all they'll achieve.

God's Word tells us, "Write the vision, and make it plain upon tables, that he may run that readeth it" (Hab. 2:2). People must have a picture or image of what they want to achieve and where they want to go. We don't think in words, we think in terms of pictures.

When Sandra and I first came to Houston we had about $500 in our pockets. We found a four-bedroom townhouse in a quiet section of town and paid for the first month's rent—which was $500! That's all we had! Some will say we were foolish, presumptuous, and mismanaging our finances. (I wouldn't suggest that anyone do this unless they are prepared to stand by their actions. Sandra and I had been building our faith for a number of years before this.) But for the four years previous to our move, we had lived in very undesirable conditions. I think I've probably seen every species of roach in North America! So

I refused to live like that again. I decided to change our surroundings. It was time to get a new image!

Please don't misunderstand me. I realize prosperity doesn't begin on the outside—it begins on the inside, within you. And I'm aware that you can live in a ghetto and be prosperous or that you can live in the most affluent part of town and be poor. But there does come a time when a person must change how they view things. If they're unemployed, they must see themselves employable and available to work. If people need a car, they need to start seeing themselves driving one! They need to start going to car dealerships and start talking cars! The greater the image, the closer that car will come to reality!

Now, when I start talking about image, some will say, "All that's fine, but I don't believe we need to have our heads in the sky." Why not? The Book of Ephesians says, "And hath raised us up together, and made us sit together in heavenly places in Christ Jesus" (2:6). Jesus identified with tax collectors, prostitutes, fishermen, and the poorest of the poor. But Jesus never forgot who He was and where He came from. This was the secret of His authority. He knew Satan had no power over Him.

> And when the tempter came to him, he said, If thou be the Son of God, command that these stones be made bread. And saith unto Him, If thou be the Son of God, cast thyself down: for it is written, He shall give his angels charge concerning thee: and in their hands they shall bear thee up, lest at any time thou dash thy foot against a stone.

And saith unto him, All these things will I
give thee, if thou wilt fall down and worship me.
—MATTHEW 4:3, 6, 9

When Satan tempted Jesus in the wilderness,
he tried to pervert the image that Jesus had of
Himself, His mission, and His ability. But Jesus
didn't bow to Satan's perverted images. Instead, He
declared the image He always confidently had.

But he answered and said, It is written, Man
shall not live by bread alone, but by every
word that proceedeth out of the mouth of
God.

Jesus said unto him, It is written again,
Thou shalt not tempt the Lord thy God.

Then saith Jesus unto him, Get thee hence,
Satan: for it is written, Thou shalt worship the
Lord thy God, and him only shalt thou serve.
—MATTHEW 4:4, 7, 10

Jesus identified with what the Word of God
said. This is what God's people must do. They
must see themselves as God sees them. God sees
us as prosperous, having abundance, giving to
the needy. He sees us helping to spread the
gospel of Jesus Christ preaching the good news
to the poor. So we must always teach people to
see themselves as the Word of God sees them.

STEP 5—TRY DIFFERENT IDEAS

His leaf also shall not wither; and whatsoever he doeth shall prosper.

—PSALMS 1:3

If we are ever going to prosper at all, we must do something! I want to handle this subject very carefully, because I have a pressing reason for this. Most people who begin in this area normally think about going into business. Most think about part-time jobs, multi-level marketing, or other variations of these things. But the best place to start is where you are! Our first business venture is to maximize the job or career we're already working in, because prosperity always begins where you are . . . not where you aren't. So ask yourself these questions:

1. Do you get to work on time?

2. Are you performing your job equal to and beyond the employer's expecta-tions?

3. Are there other positions available in your company you can aspire toward that will enable you to expand and grow?

4. Are there new and creative ideas that you can contribute to your company?

Looking for Prosperity? Look Under Your Nose

God wants to prosper us right where we are. Many times the actual vehicles we need are right under our noses. So look for them and allow God to direct you as you achieve and grow.

Many have asked me, "What about multi-level marketing?" So I tell them that multi-level marketing can range from soap products to weight-loss programs. And, I tell them that how well a person does in multi-level marketing depends on how well her or she can sell a product. Those who decide to build a multi-level business must also be successful in recruiting others to duplicate their efforts. Therefore, in my opinion, multi-level marketing is a great opportunity to launch one into financial independence—that is if he is diligent and willing to work.

But unfortunately, many people are looking for instant financial success and violate basic principles. I know of hundreds who have bought and invested in starter kits, but they never start! The only people who prosper are the ones who sold them the kit. So whatever a person decides to do, he must do it!

In any business there are low times when the business seems to be failing. So if the motive is "quick money," you will soon become discouraged. This isn't the time to give up, but to press on! There is no "easy" way to make money. All things require diligence.

But I do have a concern regarding some multi-level marketing businesses. I have been personally approached several times about a certain popular multi-level product. The marketing of this product asks those involved to attend a multitude of meetings and pep rallies, and that can get in the way of church. I realize that any business takes time to build, but I began to notice that the majority of those involved in this one certain product were missing church, Bible class, and fellowship meetings. And their only excuse was that they were "working their business."

Many even claimed that their goal was to get rich so they could give to the ministry. My main concern about this is that no believer should have to sacrifice teaching, fellowship, and worship for the purpose of making money. This is an unbalanced spiritual life. Yes, God does want us to prosper, but not at the expense of worship. Before we are called to be anything, we are called to be worshipers. God condones nothing at the expense of worship and fellowship. So always put God first, in worship and giving.

Now let me share another concern that I have. Throughout the years it has always amazed me how short-sighted we Christians can be! God is a God of creative innovation and unlimited ideas, yet we limit Him to two or three things. Notice what the Scriptures say: "Whatsoever he doeth shall prosper" (Psalm 1:3). This means exactly what it says—whatsoever! So God isn't limited to prospering through two or three specific product lines. Look at this particular scripture:

> And Esau took his wives, and his sons, and his daughters, and all the persons of his house, and his cattle, and all his beasts, and

111

all his substance, which he had got in the land of Canaan; and went into the country from the face of his brother Jacob. For their riches were more than that they might dwell together; and the land wherein they were strangers could not bear them because of their cattle.

—GENESIS 36:6–7

The Word says, "The land was not able to bear them." I believe there are some products that have reached certain levels of saturation. But this doesn't mean God can't prosper us through them. It may take longer and carry greater difficulty, but He can do it. This is where many make mistakes. They are moved by testimonies of others who have made fortunes in a particular business and they assume the type of wealth gained by those who testify of it can only be found in that particular product. But remember, God can use anything!

It is time for the believer to use his God-given creativity. There are products that have never reached certain states, gadgets that have never been invented, and services that have never been offered. So don't limit God—don't limit what He can do through people! As we search for new things, new ideas, new products, and new ways of making things work—God can receive great glory. Think about it!

STEP 6—FIND A CHRIST-CENTERED CHURCH

Finally, I can't say enough about people being

settled in a good, solid, Christ-centered church. Too often people remain in churches because they grew up there, or their parents, or grand-parents attended there. Some attend because it's close to home or they're afraid to break out of certain traditional settings. All of these reasons are admirable, but they aren't always God's will. God's will is for His children to grow up in His Word—strong and healthy. This may mean making some decisions about where a person goes to church.

We shouldn't be afraid to question the belief structure of a particular church. The Word of God is well able to make things clear as to whether a church is spiritually alive or not. Some of the signs to look for in a stable congregation include:

1. The Bible is considered to be the ulti-mate and final authority.

2. The church has a vision for the future.

3. They believe in a well-balanced view of prosperity.

4. They teach the Lordship of Jesus Christ.

5. The love of God is shown through the actions of the membership.

6. They teach the Spirit-filled and Spirit-led life.

There are other things to look for, but these six will get people started. Also remember, if people are looking for a church with no problems—encourage them to stop looking! The animal doesn't exist! Where there are people, there will be problems. But problems can be overcome, and we have been called to be overcomers!

So encourage people to find a church and plant themselves there!

> Those that be planted in the house of the
> Lord shall flourish in the courts of our God.
> —PSALMS 92:13

God's people must learn how to deal with the multitude of problems that can arise as they deal with other people. Why? Because it's people who give to other people.

> Give, and it shall be given unto you; good
> measure, pressed down, and shaken
> together, and running over, shall men give
> into your bosom. . .
> —LUKE 6:38

So we must learn to deal with people. After, all that's who Jesus died for—people. Then as we learn our lessons—as we learn to develop everything God has put within us and put the Lord first, nothing can stop us from growing into God's promised prosperity and success.

The Word of God is alive with living principles which should motivate us to act. So let's do it. Let's take responsible action. For those who will obey His word, regardless of background or culture, God guarantees wholeness in every area of life, including financial success!

So remember, management, not magic, is God's kingdom key!

CONCLUSION

In concluding this book I just want to say again that I have seen the irresponsible results of unbalanced prosperity teaching. I've seen the hurt, the disillusionment, the debt, and the lack of compassion that has sprung from the lives of those who have twisted the teaching. But I've also seen the poor, the ghettos, the financially frustrated, the unemployed, and the underemployed who could greatly benefit from hearing about God's concern for their physical needs.

Ultimately, though, it doesn't matter what you

117

or I think, what our opinion is, or what camp or school of thought we may have come from. What matters is what God says! We can't ignore an area of teaching because we disagree with or dislike the teacher. The Pauls, Apollos's and the Cephas's of our generation will always have their followers. And they won't always agree. So when it comes to the teaching of poverty and prosperity, it is the Word of God that must have the final authority.

What we share with friends and family, teach in our classes, preach from our pulpits, and instill in our families are truths that will shape the present and coming generations. But with all of the teaching, preaching, and training, it is the individual who must make the choice. So let's make sure that we give everyone we can help as much unbiased information as possible. Responsibility is the key.

> Therefore I esteem all thy precepts concerning all things to be right; and I hate every false way.
> —PSALMS 119:128

DO YOU KNOW WHO YOU ARE?

If you haven't made an inner commitment to Jesus Christ, I want to make the opportunity available to you right now. You don't have to close your eyes or wait until you go to church. Just allow me to lead you into a brand new life through the words on this page. Wherever you are now, just say the words below with me. You will be repeating the words, but you will be saying them to God. This is a prayer. Are you ready?

> *Dear God, I want You in my life. I have tried to live my life apart from You. I was wrong and I have sinned. Please forgive me. Jesus Christ, I acknowledge that You gave Your life for me. I acknowledge You have risen from the dead. You are alive. Jesus Christ, I invite You to come live in me right now. Thank you. You are now my Lord, Saviour, and King. Amen.*

My friend if you prayed this prayer with sincerity, you are now born again! And now that you are on your way to an exciting new life, would you please fill out the form on the next page and let me know so I may rejoice with you? Thank you.

Dear Ed, I have prayed with you. Please send me additional material at no cost or obligation.

Please send me your cassette tape catalog.

Name_____

Address_____

City _____ State ___ Zip _____

Mail correspondence to:

Ed Montgomery
P.O. Box 772300
Houston, Texas 77215